MESQUITE

MESQUITE
◇ COOKERY

by John "Boog" Powell

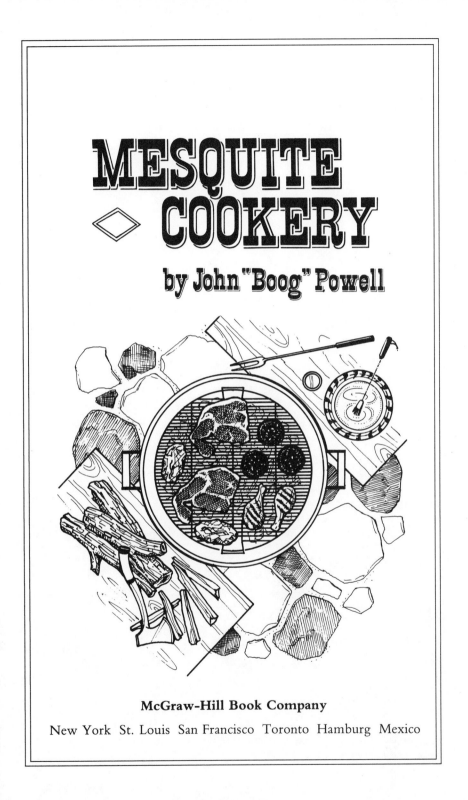

McGraw-Hill Book Company

New York   St. Louis   San Francisco   Toronto   Hamburg   Mexico

1 2 3 4 5 6 7 8 9 HAL HAL 8 7 6

ISBN 0-07-050603-5

LIBRARY OF CONGRESS CATALOGING-IN-PUBLICATION DATA

Powell, John, 1941–
  Mesquite cookery.
  Includes index.
  1. Barbecue cookery.   2. Mesquite.   I. Title.
TX840.B3P68   1986   641.7′6   85-23402

ILLUSTRATIONS BY LAURA HARTMAN
BOOK DESIGN BY PATRICE FODERO

Acknowledgments

I would like to extend my thanks to the following people for the editorial and culinary expertise that made this book possible: Jan Powell, my wife, and prime consumer of my cooking concoctions; Robert Hatchett, whose gift of mesquite started me out on my delicious hobby; Marty Blackman, my agent, whose idea it was to make my hobby into a book; Robert Chain, whose knowledge of baseball and barbecuing gave this book its birth; Linda Kilbourne, whose work in perfecting the recipes was invaluable; and Elizabeth Fox, whose work in typing the manuscript showed extraordinary patience.

Contents

Author's Note

A few years back when I first started barbecuing with mesquite it wasn't very easy to find this best of all possible outdoor cooking fuels. Apart from a few gourmet and specialty stores, mesquite wasn't that widely available in those days. But, fortunately for our renewed enthusiasm in outdoor cooking, all that has changed. With over 20 million Americans sampling mesquite cookery this year, this super-clean cooking fuel is now available either in pure form or mixed with charcoal in supermarket barbecue sections throughout the country. However, just in case you do have trouble locating high-quality mesquite for outdoor cooking I've included the name of the Lazzari Fuel Company, which has packaged and marketed the highest-grade mesquite lump charcoal for many years. With over eight shipping locations spread throughout the United States, Lazzari will ship you by U.P.S. a 15- or 40-pound bag of the highest-quality pure mesquite lump charcoal in a matter of days. Send a check or money order to: Lazzari, Box 34051, San Francisco, CA 94134.

15-pound bag—$11.95
40-pound bag—$24.95

There are ingredients called for in some of the recipes in *Mesquite Cookery* which may not be readily available in your supermarket. Almost all of these items are Asian cooking ingredients which have only recently been introduced into the American cooking mainstream. Therefore you may have to seek out a store which specializes in carrying these newly popular ingredients. You can usually find such a retail outlet by looking in the Yellow Pages under FOOD, ASIAN FOOD, or CHINESE FOOD. If this doesn't work just call your local friendly Chinese restaurant and they'll usually be glad to tell you where you can buy Chinese cooking ingredients retail. For your convenience I've included a list of the more unusual ingredients that may be called for in some of the recipes: plum sauce, hoisin sauce, hot dried red peppers, Chinese-style sesame oil, five-spice powder, oyster sauce, and Mirin, otherwise called sweet rice wine.

Introduction:
In Search of
the Perfect Barbecue

We baseball players love to eat. You may remember Babe Ruth's legendary hotdog eating sprees, or Tommy Lasorda's appetite for Chinese food. Players of America's national pastime have always been close to the "plate"—the one on the field as well as the one on the dinner table. You may be surprised to learn how many of us are actual gourmets. (Judging by the size of some of the guys, including myself, most people can see for themselves how closely associated with food we've become!)

The reasons behind this are not that hard to explain. The on-the-road life of the ball player exposes him to some of America's richest regional food treasures, so a lot of us become experts on regional cooking. In every part of the country we know where to find the most delicious regional dishes.

I was especially fortunate because for the bulk of my career I played in Baltimore, a food capital in its own right. After a game there would be no greater treat for me and my team members than digging into a plate of Baltimore's world-famous soft-shell crabs. During all-star breaks I'd drive down the Chesapeake Bay coast for the sweet corn that grows on Maryland's eastern shore. First I'd soak it, and then I'd throw it right on the grill with the crabs for the simplest of delectable feasts.

Although I was the biggest guy on my team, believe it or not, I wasn't the biggest eater. That honor went to Curt Blefary. He could pack it away. Blefary's nickname on the field was "Clanky" because of his notoriously bad hands. But in all my years with him I don't recall him dropping any food.

Many a time Clank and I celebrated at one of our favorite spots, the Gates BBQ in Kansas City. It was always super. There's probably not a ball player who played in Kansas City who hadn't been to Gates. I still can't remember the name of the street that ran behind the ballpark, even though I was the last player to hit a ball out of the stadium down that street. But what I do remember is that our team never missed going there after a game.

Another unforgettable eatery was a barbecue joint in Kansas City named the Dixieland. After we clinched the pennant in 1966, about seven or eight of us went there to celebrate—including Moe Drabowsky, Clank, Dave McNally, Andy Etchebarren and myself. Moe Drabowsky was the main character, and almost anything could happen when Drabowsky was around. (Moe was the kind of guy who would call up and order a Chinese takeout even while he

3

was warming up in the bullpen. That's not so unusual, except that Moe would call Hong Kong for his food.)

This time Moe decided to start a crap game in front of the restaurant. It was about 2 or 3 A.M. Not surprisingly, we attracted a crowd, and the game got bigger and bigger until we had about thirty or forty people rolling the dice. Just before a police paddy wagon pulled up and arrested the whole crowd I'd already hailed a cab and all of us ball players escaped in the nick of time. When you win a pennant you get the breaks.

During my years with the Orioles, I'd already become a pretty good barbecue chef and, what's more, a pretty good all-around cook. Since I'd always liked hot stuff, especially Mexican dishes, I'd learned to make my own flour and corn tortillas from scratch.

When I got into cooking, I became a perfectionist. I grew my own vegetables and was particularly proud of my peppers. About fifteen different types of chilies are now flourishing in my backyard—jalapeños, scotch bonnets (habañeros), black princes, as well as a pepper whose lineage is questionable because nobody knows what it is (and it's a killer pepper!). I grow my own oregano and basil right next to my backyard grill, so when I want to add a special flavor, all I do is reach out and throw some of these herbs on the fire.

Barbecuing came naturally to me because I grew up in Lakeland, Florida, and outdoor cooking had always been a part of my life. I learned about barbecuing as a youngster, though my early interest was mainly confined to eating the great stuff.

Those were the days when we still hadn't heard of mesquite, but that didn't stop my family from using other natural wood. During a cookout we'd all gather near the old phosphate pits just outside of Lakeland, and while we kids were swimming in the abandoned quarry my uncle Billy would dig a large cooking pit. Next he would go in search of oak wood to fill his pit. From the early morning on, Uncle Billy would carefully prepare his coals for the day's cooking.

You might say I was born and raised around a barbecue pit and that today I'm carrying this family tradition just a bit further. Buttonwood, mangrove, and sea grape woods are just some of the local natural woods I use to smoke-cook foods. But for overall everyday barbecuing, I've found that nothing compares with the quality of mesquite.

Mesquite has come a long way since the days ranchers used to hurl powerful cuss words at it for being a useless scrub tree that ate up rangeland. Thanks to the great barbecue boom, more and more of the 66 million households with barbecue grills are turning to mesquite. In city restaurants from Los Angeles to New York, diners are eager to get a taste of mesquite-cooked steak and fish and even vegetables. You can now buy mesquite in logs, chunks, chips, flakes, and charcoal. In Texas the mesquite supply business is booming. It seems everyone with a grill loves that distinctive smoky flavor that mesquite adds to cooking.

The scrubby, gnarled *Prosopis fuliflora,* as mesquite is called in the botany textbooks, has long been a part of the history of the Southwest. Indians used it for everything—as a medicine, as a food, and even as a liquor, which they made from the beans. Later on, in our century, people discovered its qualities as a wood: it has the hardness of mahogany and produces an intense heat when set ablaze. This makes it ideal for barbecuing, because the heat sears meat and seals in juices, while the smoke adds a distinctive flavor.

My first encounter with mesquite came about by accident. Since all my friends know that I am hooked on outdoor cooking, I received a call one day from a friend of mine in Texas who had a buddy in a business distributing mesquite in Florida. This entrepreneur had a big deal that went sour, and the mesquite ended up sitting in a boxcar in Florida. My friend told me that if I wanted that mesquite, all I'd have to do was to go and pick it up.

I didn't think the whole group of us Miller-Lite All-Stars could pick that sucker up, but I went out anyway and hired a truck to haul the load of mesquite wood down from Miami. Four large pallets of mesquite later, I had enough barbecue fuel to last me for years. I had so much of it that I had to use a boat barn to store the stuff. You learn how to use mesquite when you have a pile of it 30 feet high.

Once I discovered the fantastic results of barbecuing with mesquite, I wanted to find out more about this magical wood from the Southwest. To my surprise I learned that mesquite doesn't grow in just one place but is cultivated and used all over the world. In fact, lately, because of its unique cooking qualities mesquite has come of age among cooks worldwide. Even though mesquite is native to America, Italian cooks have been using it for the past 40 years. And this year alone, over 19 million Americans will join the "pros" and use mesquite for the first time!

Why do the pros use it? Simply because mesquite is a wonder-working culinary tool that burns better, longer, and hotter than other woods and adds a subtle, delicious flavor. It has a predictable flame, and because it cooks hotter you don't have to leave food on the grill as long, which means your meal won't dry out or be over-done. That, by the way, is the mark of great barbecue food. I've tried charcoals from all over the world—even eucalyptus from Australia and charcoal from Thailand—and nothing makes a better barbecue than mesquite charcoal.

I now own and manage a marina in Key West and I do plenty of entertaining. As an avid cook and sportsman, I don't always follow the rules that other chefs do. I've picked and chosen my methods, learning from others throughout my baseball travels. Now, through my affiliation with the Miller-Lite All-Stars, I've been able to enjoy some of America's best cooking. Whether it's been the Texas State-line Barbecue in Atlanta or Shorty's in Miami, I've gleaned a lot of cooking ideas just by enjoying great food.

In the pages to follow I'd like to share what I've learned over the years on the trail of the elusive perfect barbecue. What follows is not just meat from a "meaty guy." This book contains much more. Recipes for fruit and vegetable dishes, skewered treats, international delicacies, and other goodies await you. So get ready to grab your tongs, step up to the grill, and, as they say in the grand old game, "Play cook!"

1 ◇ Equipment

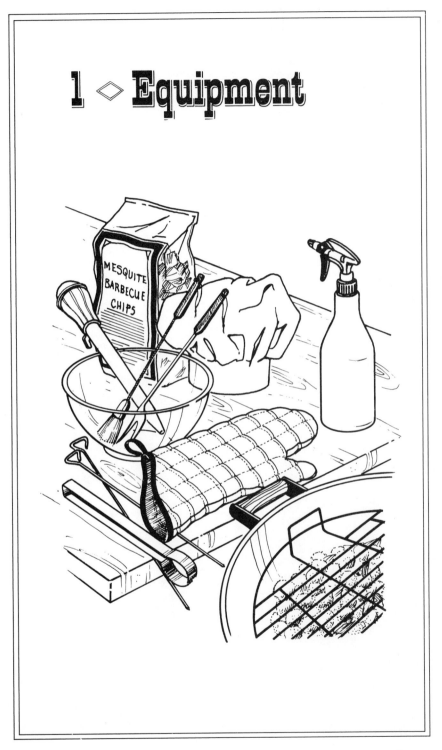

MESQUITE
BARBECUE
CHIPS

My Favorite Barbecue Tool

Ask almost any outdoor cook, "What is your favorite kind of grill?" and you can bet your bottom dollar he'll say it's the kettle grill.

The reason for that is easy to see. Because it comes in four standard sizes, the kettle grill is versatile. You can use the largest type to cook up a storm for a big whoop-de-doo, while the smallest can be taken to the campsite for a picnic.

Another one of its good features is the cover, which makes it much safer to use. As it says in the instruction booklet, you should always leave the cover on while using the grill. Some people defy this sensible rule, but remember, the cover was put there for a reason.

Despite the kettle grill's popularity, it does have one minor disadvantage. The coals are a fixed distance below the grill because neither the grill itself nor the firebox is adjustable. Some people feel this is a problem because the food is not close enough to the hot coals. It's not really a problem in my opinion, since mesquite coals need to be set no nearer than 5 inches from the grill and are plenty close enough to do a good cooking job.

All in all, kettle grills remain the most practical and easiest to use of the basic barbecue tools.

The Types of Grills

The Rectangular Grill

The two advantages of this type of cooker are its shape and its adjustability.

Since it isn't spherical, the grill is a little bit more compact, which sometimes makes it easier to handle. The adjustable grill satisfies people who like their food closer to the coals than the kettle grill allows.

There are a couple of "buts," though. First off, devoted barbecuers complain that the rectangular unit fails to spread the heat as uniformly as kettle grills. Cleaning out the ashes is also a decidedly more difficult task with rectangular grills.

Even so, if you are sold on having a rectangular grill, you may have still another difficulty: somehow they're amazingly hard to find.

The Wagon Grill

This is the "Cadillac of grills"—roomy, comfortable, dependable—and expensive! If you do a lot of grilling, however, and if you really want to be professional about it and don't mind the expense, then of all the portable charcoal grills, this may be the one for you.

What makes the wagon grill so appealing to the pros is that it usually comes fully equipped with standard features, such as an adjustable firebox and rotisseries. Along with these there are the options—for example, temperature gauges, a hood, and lights.

The Cadillac of grills, moreover, is usually built to last. Most are constructed from tough materials—some even sport *cast iron!* If you are a dedicated barbecuer, the extra money for this type of unit may be well spent.

Old-Fashioned Brick Barbecues

They're not so easy to come by these days unless you build one yourself or have one built. But for sheer volume they can't be beat.

Brick barbecues take a little more work, of course, as all old-fashioned things do. Cleaning out the ashes is, without a doubt, a real job here. Ensuring the coals give off an even heat is another. Nevertheless, there are still plenty of people who count themselves fortunate to be able to barbecue the way it was done in older times.

The Weber Kettle

This brand of grill is not as time-consuming as some of the others, where you have to keep taking the food from the grill to add fuel to feed the fire and smoke. In the Weber kettle there are openings right alongside the handles; you can use a pair of tongs to feed in live coals and extra smoking chips without disturbing the grill or the food on it.

Water Smokers

Perhaps you've seen one of these—a tall, cylindrical unit with a pan for water or other steaming liquid. Water smokers are relatively new on the market, but barbecue afficionados swear by them because the food comes out divinely juicy.

This is because the pan with the liquid (water or wine) separates the food from the heat, slowing down the cooking of the food while simultaneously enveloping it in a light smoke. Water smoking keeps the food moist and tasty.

Some people like to put aromatic herbs or a combination of orange rinds, chilies, and ginger into the liquid. You may also want to put grapevine cuttings over the coals for a really different great taste.

Water smokers are becoming extremely popular. Stores can hardly keep up with the demand. The devices come in coal, gas, and electric varieties, and as a rule they can also serve double duty as normal open grills.

But did you know that you can actually turn any covered barbecue into your own water smoker? Here's how:

1. Make a water pan from heavy-duty disposable foil, or use an old roasting pan. (It's best to wrap the pan in foil to prevent it from discoloring.)

2. Have the necessary amount of natural hardwood smoke chips available, the amount of which depends on the type of meat being smoked. Presoak chips in water for about 20 minutes while you're preparing your grill. Drain the chips and let them sit before adding to your fire.

3. If you wish, liven up your pan water with a fruity wine, citrus rinds, vinegar, or herbs. You can also put your marinade right in the pan; use a long suction baster to get at it during the cooking process.

4. Place coals around or on one side of the water pan. Start your fire. Keep it burning steadily. Gradually add just enough chips to the fire so as not to suffocate the fire. Avoid adding overly wet chips. Repeat this process every 20 to 30 minutes for a maximum smoked flavor. Every hour or so, add more mesquite to keep the fire going. Spread mesquite chunks or chips apart as you add them to prevent overcooking. (Remember, they're the hottest-burning wood around!)

5. Put the food to be cooked directly above the water so the juices will drip and collect in the pan.

6. Listen for the sizzle! When you hear it, you'll probably need to add water to the pan. You can pour it right through the grill; this way you need not displace or remove the food. But keep your pouring hand covered and protected from the steam.

Indoor Barbecuing

Unless you have a professional ventilation system for your indoor cooking, using hardwood or mesquite is not recommended. One place I do use for indoor grilling is the fireplace.

It is very easy to build a makeshift grill in your fireplace. A few red bricks and a small grill and you're set. For indoor cooking, however, mesquite gives off far too many sparks to be manageable. Sometimes a mesquite fire can get as wild as a drunken relief pitcher. That's why I use oak logs. Grilling over oak is one of life's great pleasures. It gives whatever you cook a wonderful rich flavor. However, don't go overboard by building a great big fire. If you're going to use hardwoods indoors, you should use small chunks of wood for a controlled fire.

You can also use your brick stand to cook burgers or fish or whatever by adding a wire grill basket. As with other grills, if you use a wire basket you must keep it oiled.

Timing for indoor cooking is slightly different from outdoor cooking, and only experience can be your guide for determining when something is done. Follow the basic rules I'll explain later on in Chapter 2.

Be Prepared

In baseball when you say a guy has all the tools, you know he can play. In barbecuing it means you're ready to cook.

Before you begin your barbecue feast you'll do well to get everything ready so you won't have to run back and forth fetching implements you need. First, you should make sure that your grill surface is clean. Keep it well oiled when not in use and preheat it adequately before you start cooking.

Here are some of the other tools and tricks of the trade:

- Spray bottle. Have it handy to create smoke by spraying the coals with water. Also good to have to keep the flames down.
- Fireproof mitts, not baseball mitts. Indispensable—after all, you want to cook the food, not your fingers.
- Basting brushes and suction baster. The brushes help you baste thick sauces; use the suction baster for marinades.
- Long-handled implements. Don't use forks; they put holes in your meats and vegetables. Tongs, which come in all shapes and sizes, are best. If you're especially coordinated, use chopsticks.
- Side dishes. Keep them simple. Timing is crucial when you're grilling, and you'll want to serve the whole meal at once. Remember, vegetables take a lot less time than meats if you're grilling them.

Now I'll give you the inside scoop on the most important factor of a perfect barbecue—the fire.

2 ◇ Creating a Winning Fire

Building a good mesquite fire is not something you leave to chance. For the best results you have to go about it scientifically. That means mounding your coals in a pyramid, in such a way that there is one layer of evenly burning coals underneath the food. However, you can—and should—leave an inch of empty space to spare around the perimeter of the coal pan.

The secret of this method is having just the right amount of charcoal. If you want the maximum amount of heat to focus upward, the coals must be spread to allow sufficient space between them. If your cooking is going to take long, have extra coals handy in the space near the edge; they'll be warm when you need to add them to the fire.

A lower-heat method is required for extended slow cooking or if you use a covered grill and want a sustained smoking. One way of obtaining this indirect heat is to place a drip pan of aluminum foil in the center of the grill floor immediately below the food, with coals smoldering around it. Or, if you wish the heat to be even more indirect, allowing for even slower cooking, keep the drip pan below the food but place the coals on one side of it.

I'll go into more detail about these different methods later in this chapter. First, let's work on the basics.

Starting the Grill

NOTE: Use any method you like to start your fire, *except* lighter fluid.

Newspapers, the sheets torn in half, crumpled tightly, and packed evenly on the floor of the grill, is the traditional way to get the grill fire going. Arrange the charcoals and twigs on the packed paper. Light the paper. Be sure the coals are touching one another so that the heat and fire transfers from one to the other. Then spread them according to the size of the firebox.

Some barbecuers like to use the Easy Embers Charcoal Starter, a tin container device like a large beer mug with a perforated bottom. Fill the container with charcoal, place its base on top of crumpled newspaper, and fire up the paper. After the flame has gone upward and lit the coals, empty the container into the grill.

If you don't want to bother with newspapers or other devices, then the electric fire starter may be made to order for you. After you plug the cord into an outlet, all you do is put the coil among the mesquite pieces. When the coals glow, you simply spread the pieces in the grill.

NOTE: Few things are more annoying than having a group of people watering at the mouth in anticipation of your barbecue feasts . . . and your fire is too cool! That's why it's best to start the fire about 30 to 45 minutes ahead of time and, to be on the safe side, it's better to build it too big than too small.

Hot and Cool Spots

Remember, coals that are spread out yield a cooler fire; packing coals together makes it hotter, especially with mesquite. You may want to vary the coals in hotter and cooler spots by arranging them accordingly. This gives you greater leeway in placing the food around the grill.

Safety Tips for Mesquite

Professional barbecuers know that mesquite charcoal needs to be watched, especially in its early burning stages, as it takes particular delight in shooting off sparks when it catches on fire.

Ordinary charcoal briquets pose no such problems, but with burning mesquite you should check that there are no dry grasses, leaves, or pine needles nearby that sparks could settle on. Keep your mesquite-burning grill well away from shingled roofs or any other flammable materials. It's advisable to have a garden hose or a bucket of water in the vicinity—it's better to be safe than sorry.

You'll reduce the initial flow of sparks somewhat—and actually improve mesquite's fire qualities!—if you mix hardwood chunks or chips with the mesquite charcoal. The proportion of the mix that works best is one-third mesquite to two-thirds hardwood briquets. Mesquite charcoal can also be mixed to good effect with a few other types of wood—small split fireplace logs, for example, or unsprayed fruit or nut tree chunks or chips.

Here are a few more tips concerning mesquite:

- *Never* add lighter fluid to a lighted fire or burning coals. The fire follows the stream of liquid, and if your body happens to be in the way, the results may be very unpleasant.
- Mesquite pieces are usually of uneven size. You can cut them with a hatchet into the proportion required for your particular grill.
- Always keep a squirt bottle of water near the fire in case of sudden flare-ups.

Coals: Only Use What You Need and Know When They're Ready

If you're just cooking a couple of steaks and you completely cover the floor of your firebox with mesquite, you're wasting fuel. You'd be surprised how many people are guilty of this procedure.

The question they ask is, how much is enough? And the answer is, look at your food, estimate the space it will occupy on the grill, then measure out the coals in one layer according to the size of that area (you may put in a few additional ones if you're in doubt).

If the coals are in a covered kettle and they're not directly beneath the food—what's called "indirect cooking"—the amount required should be laid out in a row about 4 inches thick along both sides of the food.

Another question that often comes up is how to tell when the coals are ready. Here you should bear in mind that a charcoal fire ranges from very hot (when the flames can be seen darting around the mesquite) to hot (the coals are bright red but there are no flames) to moderate (a whitish-gray ash covers the coals). The latter is generally the appearance coals should have for the cooking of most foods.

You can actually measure the heat of the coals by holding your hands an inch or two over the grill. If you can hold them there for 5 seconds or more, the fire is too cool to be used yet; if you can't hold them there for about 3 seconds, the fire is hot; if you can't hold them there at all the fire is obviously very hot; when the coals are covered by the whitish-gray ash, you'll be able to hold your hands over the fire without discomfort.

NOTE: If you cook fish or meats over a fire that has a red glow, chances are that the food will be overcooked. A slow fire, which is the ideal fire for cooking, has no red glow beneath the gray-white ash. As a rule, allow 30 to 45 minutes for the fire to reach the proper cooking temperature, but remember that the size and the duration of a fire vary with the type of grill, the amount and kind of food being cooked, the wind, and the charcoal being used.

Arranging the Coals for Cooking

Let's first look at covered grills. These kettle-type barbecues allow you to be flexible because you can grill, bake, roast, and partially smoke the food being cooked. Many recipes can be cooked on an open grill, but others need a covered barbecue.

Arranging the coals in a covered grill can be done in several ways. You can mound the coals directly under the food, cooking with the cover on. Or you can place the coals to the sides of the grill, which means that they're not directly under the food, so you may want to use a drip pan in order to catch the juices. Here, too, however, you cook with the cover on.

The rule of thumb for the latter indirect method is that you employ it for foods that require cooking for *more than 25 minutes*. In this case, placing the coals to the sides of the covered grill makes sense, because during this length of time you would not want to keep turning over your food again and again so as to prevent it from getting too charred.

The Covered Grill Uncovered

It is, of course, possible to use your covered grill with the top open and the food directly above the coals. Weber, America's biggest maker of covered grills, discourages this practice, however. It points out that using the grill in this manner defeats the purpose for which the covered kettle grill was designed. The problem with using the covered grill uncovered is that the fire needs to be more than ordinarily hot when both the grill and firebox are stationary and the grill is 5 inches from the coals.

Uncovered Grills

Unlike the covered grill, here you have no choice but to grill directly over the coals. This presents advantages and disadvantages. The advantage is that food grilled in the traditional open manner has a juicy, tender inside while the outside, being slightly charred, has a nice, crunchy taste. The disadvantage is that it's hard to regulate the fire, which is likely to leap up—especially with fatty foods.

There is, however, a method of using uncovered barbecues that allows you to grill with varying cooking temperatures. It's a question of arranging the coals. Rather than laying out the coals uniformly, leave bunches of coals closely packed together—kind of like islands spread evenly with little spaces between them and the rest of the coals.

Now you have a grill that enables you to cook with two different temperatures: hot and hotter. You'll find this especially useful when you're cooking up a big batch of food items, steaks, pieces of chicken, or chops. It even works well with hamburgers.

What's so nifty about this method is that it allows you to use the really hot spots to concentrate the juices while you continue cooking in the cooler areas. You simply rearrange the food items on the grill according to whether they're cooking too slowly or too fast.

Facts about Mesquite and Lump Charcoal

There are barbecue enthusiasts who claim they won't use anything but lump charcoal. They say that it creates a hotter fire and that as a result the juices of foods like chicken, fish, or meat concentrate better. To these afficionados, briquets don't have the right odor because of the coal and other elements contained in them.

There is a lot to be said for these claims in favor of lump charcoal. The only problem is that lump charcoal costs more and is not obtainable everywhere. In addition, the pieces are uneven in size, and you may have to use a hatchet to chop them into lumps suitable for your grill.

Bearing in mind the safety precautions mentioned earlier, you can avoid the controversy of lump charcoal versus briquets by using mesquite, known for its high heat and unique aromatic smoke. Mesquite is superior to briquets if you want a fire that starts out hotter than that produced by briquets. Mesquite is also the charcoal of choice if you're grilling foods that require a longer time to cook—a roast or ribs, for instance—because it stays hot longer than briquets.

NOTE: Mesquite *wood* has a stronger aroma than mesquite charcoal; the latter is recommended, as the odor of the former may overpower some foods.

Recycle Your Coals

We're all energy-conscious these days, and the same goes for your barbecue. On a covered grill, close the top and bottom air ducts once your food has been cooked. In an open grill, you may mist the coals with water when you're done cooking. With these methods some people manage to use the same mesquite charcoal, especially if they were using larger lumps, as many as three times. Remember, though, that used coals do not start up as quickly and their heat is not quite as hot. Therefore, the practical way to recycle is to mix used with fresh charcoal when you start your grill.

When It's Done

Grilling, like any skill, takes know-how. You need tools, equipment, and knowledge. But as the old saying goes, the proof is in the pudding—in this case, in the taste of your barbecued foods. Here the crucial question is knowing exactly when something is done. There are no gadgets to help you with this test. You need to use your three senses: touch, sound, and smell.

- Touch. Still the best way of knowing when something is done cooking. Steaks, chops, and chicken (especially breast meat) reveal their secrets of optimum doneness to your fingertips. Of course, this is not the preferred method when you have guests who may be squeamish about hygiene. In that event, use the bottom of a long-handled fork (not the tines). With a little practice, you can become as expert about the state of the cooked food using this method as using your fingertips. (For comparison, press on the uncooked meat before you put it on the grill.)

- Sound. Not the most reliable test, but still one that's useful. When you hear a sputtering sound, you're likely to find that the food needs more cooking. A hearty sizzle is an indicator that you may want to keep an eye on the food, as it may be getting close to being done. If there's *no* noise, you're likely to find that the food is not cooking at all.

- Smell. Again, not altogether dependable, but helpful. To the experienced nose, a raw steam smells different from a cooked one. Between these two extremes is the range of aromas that tells you how far the food has progressed in being cooked. Professional barbecue cooks have a knack of opening the cover of the grill, sticking their nose in the smoke, and pronouncing judgment. That takes some experience and practice, however.

In my recipes, I've provided basic time recommendations for each dish. But since a barbecue fire, unlike an oven, provides a variable amount of heat, you'll also have to use the three senses I just told you about for best results.

3 ◇ Aromatic Techniques

What's the most satisfying thing about barbecuing? The great taste of the food, naturally. But another element that lifts the hearts of grill users almost as much is the aroma of that steak or hamburger sizzling on the coals. After all, that light, smoky smell makes the food taste so good.

The easiest way to obtain that coveted aroma is to dash about a handful of fresh aromatic leaves straight onto the coals while the food's on the grill. Bay leaves, for example, make a great aromatic smoke. This technique has been used for centuries in Mediterranean countries.

A similar result can be achieved by throwing fruit stems or fruitwood cuttings, grapevine cuttings, even juniper twigs, a handful or so, onto the coals. Herbs, especially woody perennial varieties, also do a remarkable job in giving your smoke that tangy touch. Sage, thyme, rosemary, or tarragon are particularly recommended.

There's yet another way in which you may want to use herbs to liven up the taste of grilled foods. Just take a little cluster of fresh herbs, tie them together, and make them into a basting brush. Dip this brush into melted butter or olive oil for basting the food on the grill.

WARNING: We've living in an age of sprays, pesticides, herbicides, and chemical additives. So if you use stem cuttings or plant leaves, be certain that they haven't been recently sprayed. And always rinse them thoroughly anyway.

Here are some handy hints when you're using aromatics:

- If you're using aromatic woods while cooking on an indoor fire, you *must* have an absolutely first-class ventilation system! In fact, it should be at least as good as the ventilation system in a restaurant. Even outdoors, though they love the savory smell, a lot of people choose to keep away from the smoke while the food is on the grill.

- To get that supersmoky taste on an open grill, do this: use wood chips or vine cuttings that are somewhat moist; make a cover for the grill from heavy-duty aluminum foil—but don't cut off the air supply to the coals!

- Mesquite and hickory woods—dry or moist—add a pronounced taste to your barbecue foods. They go well with

27

solid foods, such as beef, pork, and some seafoods. For a taste of Southern-style cooking, hickory wood will provide that wonderful sweet-smoky flavor.

- To get the same results in home cooking that restaurants do with mesquite, you may find that you'll need to get some practice in supplying the steady draft this kind of charcoal requires.

- In Mediterranean France or Italy grapevine cuttings have been added to fires by generations of cooks to lend a subtly sweet seasoning to grilled fish, chicken, lamb, vegetables, and veal. Dry grapevines will raise the heat of the fire at first, then give off a wispy, delicately scented smoke.

- A whole range of different delicate flavors can be obtained by throwing fresh herbs, such as dill or garlic, citrus rinds, or fruit wood chips directly on your grill fire.

- When recipes call for grapevines, you may find it easier to find fruit wood scraps (such as apple or elder) instead; these chips, however, are not available everywhere. Walnut or aspen can also be used, if available.

The latest barbecue innovation is called "smoke chips." These chips are not charcoal, but pieces of actual hardwood which produce aromatic smoke. Besides smoke chips, some manufacturers are marketing woods such as mesquite, hickory, maple, cherry, and oak that have been shredded, chunked, or chipped.

Hardwood Smoking

You should remember that mesquite and other hardwood charcoals burn far hotter than hardwood chunks. But the hardwood chunks give off a stronger aroma and make for a more flavorful barbecue than their charcoal counterparts. Keep in mind that wood chunks go best with strongly flavored foods, such as game, oily fish, pork, and lamb. More delicate kinds of food, such as lean fish and poultry, can be overpowered by the strongly aromatic wood chunks. You'll see the differences at once if you try cooking fish over a fire of mesquite wood chunks and then compare it with fish cooked over mesquite charcoal: the former will have a much stronger smoky taste than the latter. On the other hand, the heat given off from the coals of hickory or mesquite chunks is exactly what's needed to cook some foods, such as barbecued ribs, to perfection.

And don't forget that if you want to squeeze every aromatic particle from your hardwood chunks, a covered grill is the way to go. With an open grill much of that precious smoke will be dispersed into the air.

Here's the best way to make hardwood chunks smoke long and slow. Before adding chunks to the fire, take aluminum foil and wrap each piece individually and tightly. Next, take a pin and make tiny holes all over the foil. When all are ready, throw the pieces on a hot fire. Watch how the smoke escapes ever so slowly through the holes.

Here are a few other sure-fire hints for getting the most out of your wood or chips:

- About 15 to 20 minutes before your fire is ready, begin soaking your wood chunks, chips, or twigs, so that when you put them in the fire pan they won't burn, but smolder.

- For big items like turkeys or roasts, use four to six *pieces* of wood (about 1 quart of chips). I use a 1-pound coffee can for convenient measuring. For smaller items, use about half that amount. 1 quart chips = 2 coffee cans filled.

- Be sure to keep additional chips soaking. You can never be certain of the amount of smoke that escapes when you raise the lid or through other variables.

IMPORTANT: Do not use wood chips from evergreen trees like pine or cedar. A pitch or resin flavor is not what you want.

4 ◇ Marinades

Mexican Chili Paste ◇ Garlic and Mint Marinade ◇ Ginger
Marinade ◇ K.I.S.S. (Keep It Simple, Stupid) Marinade ◇
Lemon-Herb Marinade ◇ Lime-Orange Marinade ◇
Mustard-Herb Marinade ◇ Orange Marinade for Fowl ◇ Pork
Marinade ◇ Rib 'n' Beer Marinade ◇ Teriyaki Marinade ◇
Simple Wine Marinade ◇ Red Wine Marinade ◇
Indian Yogurt Marinade

◇

There is no question in my mind that anything tastes better cooked in smoke over a mesquite fire. But, everything else being equal, what distinguishes the taste of one piece of meat or chicken from another? Without a doubt, the spices and tenderizers of the marinades you use are the most important factors.

So it shouldn't come as a surprise that most of my own favorite grilled specialties begin with a number of these versatile flavoring agents. In a great many barbecued dishes that evoke the wonder of my guests I credit my success to what I call M&M—mesquite and marinade.

The flavor-giving richness of the marinade is no secret. Marinades are used in cooking all over the world and can be found in a sweet teriyaki type of flavor or the more pungent garlic and mint marinade that goes especially well with lamb and more "gamey" dishes.

I described marinades as versatile, and they truly are. Once you have learned the basics of preparing marinades, you can use your own creative talents to give grilled foods the flavor accents you prefer.

It's really very simple. The wonderful thing about marinades is that you need no more than a little red wine, a bottle of beer, or a cup of vinegar for the basic "brew." Then let your beef, chicken, or fish soak in the flavors of your choice. Just add a dash of sugar, your favorite spice, a pinch of salt and pepper, and presto!—*your marinade will be ready to give zing to most grilled meats.*

◇ *Mexican Chili Paste*

6 to 8 dried red chilies (available at Mexican and Latin-Amer-
ican specialty stores) or 8 tbsp ground chili powder
½ tsp dried oregano
2 tbsp sweet red wine
¼ tsp ground cumin
¼ tsp ground black pepper
2 tbsp white vinegar
3 garlic cloves, crushed
juice of 1 lemon and 1 lime
salt to taste

First remove the seeds and veins from the chilies. Then cut the chilies into small pieces and soak them in one cup warm water for about 30 minutes or until they begin to swell. Remove the chilies and reserve the water. Add chilies to a blender along with remaining ingredients. Blend only for a few seconds until mixture turns into a chunky texture. To thin, add to the paste 1 or 2 tablespoons of the water in which the chilies were soaked. If ground chili powder is used, use 2 tablespoons of water. Then mix with a fork to avoid too smooth a texture.

(Makes 1 cup)

◇ *Garlic and Mint Marinade*

¼ cup mint leaves, fresh or dry
1 bay leaf, shredded
4 garlic cloves, crushed
⅓ cup peanut oil
½ cup red wine vinegar
4 tbsp sherry
2 tbsp soy sauce

Chop the mint finely and combine with shredded bay leaf. Mix in the remaining ingredients in a large bowl. Place meat in marinade for several hours, turning occasionally. Drain the meat before placing on the grill.

(Makes 1 cup)

◇ *Ginger Marinade*

1 cup green onions
½ cup peanut oil
½ cup soy sauce
½ cup dry sherry or mirin (sweet rice wine)
¼ cup fresh ginger, grated
1 tbsp brown sugar
¼ cup cilantro (optional)

Chop the green onions into very small pieces. Combine the remaining ingredients in a bowl or jar and mix thoroughly. Pour ingredients into a marinating dish and add the chopped green onions. Mix gently, allowing the green onions to float on the surface of marinade as much as possible. This marinade is great for shellfish.

(Makes 2 cups)

◇ *K.I.S.S. (Keep It Simple, Stupid) Marinade*

1 onion, finely diced
1 garlic clove, crushed
1 cup Miller Lite Beer
½ cup peanut or olive oil

Dice the onion and crush the garlic. Mix together with beer and oil until well blended. Use with shrimp or beef.

(Makes 1½ cups)

◇ *Lemon-Herb Marinade*

½ tsp dried rosemary
½ tsp dried tarragon
½ tsp dried thyme

½ cup olive oil
2 tbsp grated lemon rind
1 cup lemon juice

Combine all ingredients except lemon juice in a small saucepan. Cook over medium heat 3 to 5 minutes, so that spices release their flavor and mix into oil. Remove from heat, adding juice. Bring mixture to room temperature. This marinade is a general all-purpose one that should be made ahead of time and stored in refrigerator.

(Makes 1½ cups)

◇ *Lime-Orange Marinade*

4 garlic cloves, finely chopped
1½ cups lime juice
1 cup orange juice
½ cup peanut oil
2 tsp ground black pepper
salt
4 bay leaves

Chop garlic and mix with remaining ingredients in a bowl. Marinate ribs, chops, or thick cuts of beef with this tangy, spicy combination. Always try to use fresh juices. When they're not readily available, use the frozen or bottled variety.

(Makes 3 cups)

◇ *Mustard-Herb Marinade*

½ cup Dijon mustard
2 tbsp dry mustard
2 tbsp vegetable oil
¼ cup dry white wine
2 tbsp dried tarragon
2 tbsp dried thyme
2 tbsp dried sage, crushed

Mix all of the ingredients in a bowl. Let stand 1 hour. Add chicken or fish and coat well. Let stand in marinade. Pat dry with paper towels. Use the remaining marinade to baste fish or chicken just before removing from the grill.

(Makes 1 cup)

◇ *Orange Marinade for Fowl*

½ cup brandy
1 cup fresh orange juice
1 tsp fresh ginger, grated, or 1 tsp dried ginger
1 tsp dried tarragon
3 tbsp orange liqueur
salt
1 tsp black pepper

First rub fowl—either chicken, duck, or game hens—with one-fourth of the brandy. Mix remaining brandy, orange juice, liqueur, salt, pepper, ginger, and tarragon. Pour over bird and let marinate. Also use marinade to baste while grilling.

(Makes 1½ cups)

◇ *Pork Marinade*

½ cup soy sauce
¼ cup peanut oil
¼ cup vinegar
1 tbsp molasses or 2 tbsp brown sugar
2 tbsp rosemary, crushed
1 tsp dried ginger
1 tsp dry mustard
1 tsp salt
2 garlic cloves, minced

Combine all ingredients in a bowl. Beat the marinade with a whisk so flavors combine. This is the simplest method to prepare a flavorful pork marinade for grilling.

(Makes 1 cup)

◇ Rib 'n' Beer Marinade

1 qt Miller Lite Beer
2 cups brown sugar
1 cup cider vinegar
1 tbsp chili powder
1 tsp ground cumin
1 tsp dry mustard
2 tsp hot red pepper, crushed
2 bay leaves
6 slabs pork baby back ribs (about 1½ lb each)
½ cup ketchup

Combine beer, sugar, vinegar, spices, and bay leaves in a large pan. Bring to a boil, remove from heat, and cool. Place ribs in a large, shallow roasting pan. Pour marinade over ribs. Turn ribs several times while they marinate about 24 hours in refrigerator. Drain ribs, reserving marinade. Arrange ribs on grill or rib rack and smoke-cook 2 to 3 hours, or in a smoker 6 to 7 hours, until meat is tender, basting with the marinade 20 to 30 minutes. When meat is tender, brush with a little ketchup. This marinade goes well with any meat that is going to be smoked and grilled.

(Makes 3½ cups)
(Serves 6–8)

◇ Teriyaki Marinade

1 tbsp sesame oil
¼ cup pineapple juice or 4 tbsp brown sugar
½ cup orange juice
¼ cup soy sauce
2 tbsp lemon juice
4 tbsp sugar
1 bay leaf
2 tsp dried ginger
2 tbsp dry vermouth or sweet rice wine
1 small garlic clove, crushed

Mix all the ingredients in a jar. Use on beef, chicken, and pork. To give grilled meats an added glaze, use 1½ times the amount of sugar called for and baste frequently during grilling so that marinade caramelizes on meats.

(Makes 1 cup)

◇ *Simple Wine Marinade*

> ½ cup vegetable oil
> ½ cup red or white wine
> 2 tsp red or white wine vinegar
> 2 tsp onion, finely grated
> 1 garlic clove, minced
> 1½ tsp salt
> 1 tsp Tabasco sauce

Combine all ingredients in a jar. Shake vigorously and cover tightly. Store marinade in refrigerator a few days. Before using, bring to room temperature and shake marinade well. Meats marinate better in this kind of mixture when they are placed in marinade at room temperature.

(Makes 1 cup)

◇ *Red Wine Marinade*

> 3 cups dry red wine
> grated rind and juice of 2 lemons
> 2 bay leaves
> 2 whole cloves
> 1 tbsp fresh-ground black pepper
> 1 large onion, sliced
> 3 carrots, chopped
> 3 celery stalks, finely chopped
> 3 garlic cloves, crushed
> 1 tsp thyme

1 tsp tarragon
1 tbsp sugar
1 tsp salt

This marinade is especially flavorsome with larger cuts of meat. Place a roast or other large piece of beef in a bowl. Combine ingredients and pour over beef. Cover and refrigerate overnight, turning several times. Remove meat and drain. Place meat on grill over a low mesquite flame and smoke for 3 to 4 hours. When meat is grilled, use marinade to brush over slices of the beef.

(Makes 3½ cups)

◇ *Indian Yogurt Marinade*

2 garlic cloves, minced
1 tbsp fresh ginger, finely grated, or 1 tsp dried ginger
2 tbsp vegetable oil
1 tsp ground cardamom
½ tsp ground cumin
1 tsp dried, ground coriander seed
paprika, for coloring
½ tsp ground turmeric
⅛ tsp cayenne (or more to taste)
1 cup yogurt
½ tsp salt

Mix all ingredients into a small bowl. Season to taste. Use with chicken and lamb. The tenderizing effect of this marinade is much greater if you allow the meat to sit in marinade overnight in the refrigerator.

(Makes 1 cup)

5 ◇ Sauces

Spicy Almond Sauce ◇ Beer Barbecue Sauce ◇ French Butter
Sauce ◇ Herb Butters ◇ Cherry Glaze for Grilled Ham Steaks
◇ Green Chili Sauce ◇ Chimi-Churri ◇ Chinese Barbecue
Sauce ◇ Citrus Sauce for Fish ◇ Memphis-Style Dry Barbecue
Seasoning ◇ Hawaiian-Style Glaze for Ham Steak ◇ Spicy Lime
Sauce ◇ Hot Mint Sauce ◇ Old-Fashioned Barbecue Sauce ◇
Thai Peanut Sauce ◇ Simple Salsa ◇ Spicy Barbecue Sauce for
Seafood ◇ Sweet and Sour Sauce for Dipping ◇ Polynesian
Teriyaki Sauce ◇ Sweet Wine Basting Sauce for Chicken

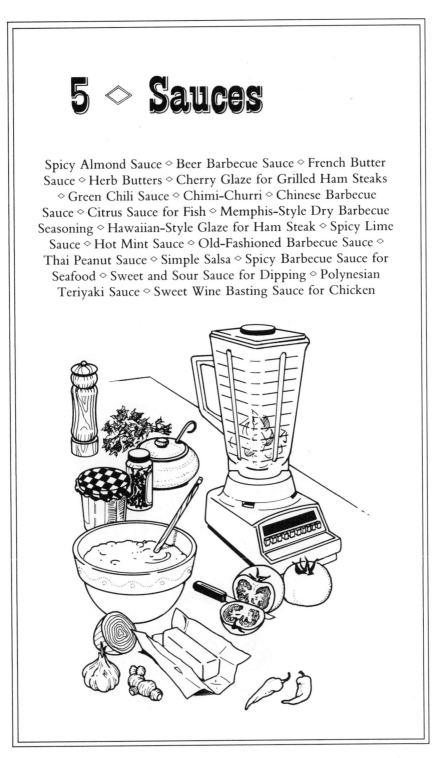

◇

If you were to set out as a globe-trotting gourmet, you'd be most impressed with the diversity of sauces in the world. Whatever type of cooking you were sampling, in whatever part of the world, you'd find that the sauces are what makes each cuisine unique.

Take our own American kitchen. Here, too, different sauces highlight the specialties of each region. The South offers us the peppery and pungent sensations of sauces native to New Orleans. The spicy barbecue sauces of Texas are legendary. Equally renowned are the chili-based sauces of the Southwest. In the West, there is a veritable wealth of sauces, brought to our Pacific shores by people who have settled there from the Asian nations.

The way I look at it, the sauce—whether a glaze or a dipping variety—is like the paint on a house. The house itself may be sound and architecturally pretty, but without the complementary paint it would fail to please the eye. Similarly, it's the sauce that gives the dish its special flavor, making it a pleasure to the palate.

Food gets an added flavor boost from sauces. A good sauce can be used on many different types of food. What's more, the right kind of sauce can help to make up for food that hasn't been cooked to its maximum flavor potential on the grill. Even if you've charred your food a little too much, with some of these sauces at the ready, you'll have a feast you can be proud of!

◇ Spicy Almond Sauce

⅓ cup almonds
1 tbsp butter or oil
1 garlic clove, crushed
½ tsp cayenne pepper or ¾ tsp Tabasco sauce
1 small tomato, peeled and seeded
1 cup olive oil
2 tbsp red wine vinegar
salt

Toast the almonds until lightly browned in frying pan with 1 tablespoon butter or oil and drain. Combine with garlic, cayenne pepper, tomato and 1 tablespoon of olive oil, and blend to a smooth paste. Then, with the motor running, add the remaining oil slowly to maintain a paste. Add vinegar and salt to taste.

(Makes 1½ cups)

◇ Beer Barbecue Sauce

1½ cups ketchup
12 oz Miller Lite Beer
½ cup brown sugar
¼ cup red wine vinegar
1 tsp dry mustard
1 tsp dry basil
1 tsp red pepper
2 tsp prepared French mustard
1 tbsp Worcestershire sauce

Combine all above ingredients in a medium saucepan, and bring to a boil. Reduce heat, cover, and simmer for about 30 minutes. Then, approximately 10 minutes before using, simmer sauce uncovered so it will thicken slightly.

(Makes about 3 cups)

◇ *French Butter Sauce*

¼ *cup minced shallots*
¼ *cup dry white wine*
¼ *cup fresh lemon juice*
1 *cup unsalted butter*

This classic sauce is especially useful for adding richness to grilled fish. Combine the shallots, wine, and lemon juice. Then, preferably in a nonstick pan, bring mixture to a boil, and reduce until about half of the liquid boils off and the mixture begins to darken. Avoid scorching. Let the mixture cool, and add about 2 tbsp of butter, stirring steadily until butter melts and blends into mixture. Return the pan to a low flame, and add the remaining butter, 1 tablespoon at a time, stirring carefully to mix the butter with the liquid. This gradual process will create a creamier butter sauce. To prevent separation, remove the sauce from the flame and beat with a whisk.

Variations: Substitute red wine and red wine vinegar to make an elegant, pink French butter sauce. For an Asian taste add 1 tbsp fresh ginger. Let your imagination be your guide: use dill, basil, cilantro, or tarragon to vary the flavor of grilled foods such as chicken and fish.

(Makes ½ cup)

◇ *Herb Butters*

4 *tbsp unsalted butter*
1 *tbsp fresh parsley, finely chopped*
1½ *tsp shallots, finely minced*
rind of ¼ *lemon, minced*
salt and pepper
2 *tsp lemon juice*

Have the butter at room temperature, and whisk to a smooth, frothy consistency. Add remaining ingredients, and beat until completely combined. Set aside and permit flavors to blend. Serve generous dollops on grilled fish, chicken, and steaks.

Variations: For an Italian accent mix in a crushed garlic clove and 2 to 3 tablespoons of fresh, finely chopped basil. For a Southwestern flavor mix in 2 teaspoons chili powder, ½ clove crushed garlic, 1 pinch of crushed oregano, 1 pinch of ground cumin, 1 teaspoon finely grated lime peel. Additional flavors that mix well as herb butters include: cilantro and garlic; lime and ginger; or cayenne pepper, black pepper, and white pepper.

(Makes ⅛ cup)

◇ *Cherry Glaze for Grilled Ham Steaks*

1 1-lb can pitted cherries
2 tbsp cornstarch
¾ cup red wine
2 tbsp rum
2 tbsp wine vinegar
¼ cup sugar
2 tbsp lemon juice

Drain and reserve cherries. Add cherry juice to cornstarch, and mix well, eliminating lumps until mixture is smooth. Add wine, rum, vinegar and sugar. Bring mixture to a boil, stirring continually to maintain a smooth sauce. Mix in lemon juice. Brush ½ cup of glaze on ham steaks before grilling. When the ham is ready to serve, add cherries to remaining sauce and heat slowly. Serve each ham steak with a generous portion of cherry glaze.

(Makes 2 to 3 cups)

◇ *Green Chili Sauce*

2 oz fresh green chilies (serrano, jalapeño, etc.), seeded, deveined, and finely chopped
¼ cup vinegar
2 tbsp cilantro, finely chopped
1 garlic clove, crushed
salt to taste

Combine all ingredients in a blender or food processor, and blend until smooth. Serve at room temperature over fish or chicken.

(Makes ½ cup)

◇ *Chimi-Churri*

> ½ cup olive oil
> ¼ cup red wine vinegar
> ¼ cup pimentos, finely diced
> 1 garlic clove, crushed
> 1 large onion, finely diced
> 1 bunch parsley, finely chopped
> 1 bunch cilantro, finely chopped
> 1 tsp dried oregano
> ¼ tsp cayenne pepper
> 1½ tsp salt
> 1 tsp coarsely ground pepper

Mix all the ingredients together and let stand. Use as a marinade for steaks. Brush on steaks just before removing the meat from the grill. A dollop goes well as a relish with most types of grilled steaks.

(Makes about 1½ cups)

◇ *Chinese Barbecue Sauce*

> ¾ cup plum sauce or hoisin sauce
> ¾ cup ketchup
> ½ tsp dry mustard
> 2 tsp honey
> ½ tsp cayenne pepper
> 1 tsp sesame oil
> ½ bottle (6 oz) Miller Lite Beer
> 1 garlic clove, crushed
> 1 tsp fresh ginger, finely chopped

First drink half a bottle of Miller Lite. Combine all the ingredients in a skillet or saucepan. Bring to a boil, reduce heat, and simmer until the sauce thickens. If you like a hotter sauce you can add slightly more cayenne pepper. Bring to room temperature, and use as a glaze for ribs and chicken or as an all-purpose dipping sauce.

(Makes 1½ cups)

◇ *Citrus Sauce for Fish*

>   1 cup water
>   ¼ cup lime juice
>   ½ cup soy sauce
>   ¼ cup orange marmalade
>   3 tbsp cornstarch
>   ¼ cup water
>   1½ tsp finely grated lemon rind

Bring water, lime juice, soy sauce, and marmalade to a gentle boil until marmalade dissolves. Mix 3 tablespoons of cornstarch with the remaining ¼ cup of water, and add to the mixture. Return mixture to a gentle boil until it thickens. Add lemon rind and stir. Remove from heat, and let stand until the sauce reaches room temperature.

(Makes 2 cups)

◇ *Memphis-Style Dry Barbecue Seasoning*

>   1 tbsp garlic powder
>   1 tbsp onion powder
>   1 tbsp white pepper
>   1 tbsp black pepper
>   1 tbsp chili powder
>   1 tbsp ground red pepper
>   1 tbsp cumin
>   2 tbsp paprika

Mix all ingredients in a bowl. Pour into a salt shaker. Sprinkle lightly on ribs or chops during grilling for "dry" barbecue flavor. Once ribs are ready, shake seasoning over meat to taste and serve. Use this method along with barbecue sauces for an extra spicy effect.

(Makes ½ cup)

◇ *Hawaiian-Style Glaze for Ham Steak*

¾ cup honey
¾ cup pineapple juice
½ tsp dry mustard
1 tbsp fresh ginger, finely grated
3 whole cloves

Place ingredients in a saucepan, and reduce by stirring over low flame until it reaches a syrupy consistency. Spread this glaze over the ham shortly before removing it from the grill. Prevent burning of the glaze by paying careful attention to the final moments of grilling.

(Makes 1 cup)

◇ *Spicy Lime Sauce*

¼ cup peanut oil
¼ cup vinegar
1 clove garlic, minced
½ tsp salt
1 tsp rosemary
1 tsp grated horseradish
¼ cup lime juice
½ tsp grated lime rind

Place all above ingredients into a jar or blender. Cover and blend or shake well. Place in refrigerator and let stand for several hours, or make sauce the night before using. Shake well before serving. Use as a sauce or a marinade.

(Makes about ¾ cup)

◇ *Hot Mint Sauce*

½ cup chicken stock
½ cup white wine vinegar
⅛ cup sugar
¾ cup fresh mint leaves, finely chopped
½ tsp dried red peppers, crushed

Pour chicken stock, vinegar, and sugar into a saucepan. Bring this broth to a boil until sugar dissolves. Chop the mint leaves. Blend the hot broth with the crushed chili peppers and the chopped mint leaves, setting aside 1 tablespoon of chopped mint leaves. Let stand until mixture cools, and then pour through a strainer. Return this mixture to the pan and simmer over a low flame until the liquid has a syrupy consistency. Cool to room temperature and sprinkle in remaining chopped mint before serving.

(Makes 1 cup)

◇ *Old-Fashioned Barbecue Sauce*

  4 cups ketchup
  ½ cup ground mustard
  ½ cup cider vinegar
  ⅛ cup honey
  ½ cup Worcestershire sauce
  2 tbsp Tabasco sauce
  ½ cup horseradish
  2 tsp salt
  1 tsp black pepper, freshly ground
  1 tbsp sugar
  1 garlic clove, crushed
  1 tsp sage

Combine all ingredients in a saucepan. Bring to a boil while stirring constantly. Set aside and let cool to room temperature. Use for basting spareribs and as a general-purpose barbecue sauce for hamburgers, pork, etc.

(Makes 5 cups)

◇ *Thai Peanut Sauce*

   1 cup onion, finely chopped
¼ cup garlic, minced
   1 tsp ground cumin
⅓ cup fresh ginger, finely grated
   2 tbsp dried hot red pepper, crushed
¼ cup peanut oil
⅓ cup soy sauce
   3 tbsp cider vinegar
½ cup coconut milk or coconut cream
   1 cup chunky peanut butter
¼ cup cilantro, finely chopped

In a blender puree the onion, garlic, cumin, ginger, red pepper. Heat the oil in a pan over low heat. Add puree to the pan, and sauté over low heat for 5 to 7 minutes. Combine the remaining ingredients in a bowl and blend thoroughly. Add this mixture to the pan, while stirring continually to prevent sticking. Cover pan and simmer until sauce thickens. Remove from the fire and stir in fresh chopped cilantro. Set aside until the sauce cools to room temperature. Serve with grilled beef, pork, or chicken.

(Makes 2½ cups)

◇ *Simple Salsa*

   4 large tomatoes
   1 onion, finely chopped
   2 or 3 serrano chilies, seeded, deveined, and very finely minced
¼ cup cilantro, finely minced
   1 large garlic clove, finely minced
salt to taste

Remove skin from tomatoes. (Dip them in boiling water for about 30 seconds to 1 minute, then run them under cold water; skins will just slip off.) Set aside to cool. Then dice tomatoes, and add minced chilies, cilantro, garlic, and salt to taste. Mix well. Salsa is more flavorful when made 1 or 2 hours ahead of time.

(Makes 1½ cups)

◇ *Spicy Barbecue Sauce for Seafood*

1 cup sour cream
1 cup mayonnaise
2 garlic cloves, crushed
¼ cup parsley, finely chopped
1 tsp salt
3 tbsp sweet relish
1 tbsp Worcestershire sauce
1 tbsp tarragon, freshly chopped, or 1 tsp dried tarragon, crushed
1 tsp dry mustard
1 tsp paprika
½ tsp cayenne pepper
1 tsp Tabasco sauce
1 tsp vinegar

Combine all ingredients and blend well. Serve as a dipping sauce for shellfish, or top off grilled fish steaks with dollops.

(Makes 2 cups)

◇ *Sweet and Sour Sauce for Dipping*

¼ cup shallots, minced
¼ cup garlic, crushed
1 tbsp hot dried red pepper
1 tbsp peanut oil
¼ cup oyster sauce
1 tbsp brown sugar
¼ cup water
2 tsp soy sauce
2 scallions, minced
1 tbsp cilantro, finely chopped

In a skillet sauté shallots, garlic, and red pepper in peanut oil until browned. Stir lightly to prevent burning. Remove from heat and set aside. Combine oyster sauce, sugar, water, soy sauce and sautéed spice mixture in a saucepan. Bring to a boil, stirring continually until sugar is thoroughly dissolved. Remove sauce from heat. Stir in scallions and cilantro, and bring to room temperature. Serve as dipping sauce for grilled fish, chicken, or kabobs.

(Makes about ¾ cup)

◇ *Polynesian Teriyaki Sauce*

½ cup teriyaki sauce
⅓ cup apricot preserves
½ tsp fresh ginger, finely grated
2 garlic cloves, crushed
1 tbsp cornstarch
¼ cup cold water

Combine first four ingredients in a pan. Bring mixture to a slow boil, and remove from fire. Then mix the cornstarch in cold water until dissolved. Return the pan with the sauce to a low flame. Add the cornstarch, stirring the sauce until it thickens. Serve over steaks, chicken, and fish.

(Makes ¾ cup)

◇ *Sweet Wine Basting Sauce for Chicken*

1 cup rosé or sweet red wine
1 tsp dried rosemary, crushed
½ tsp fresh ginger, finely chopped
1 tsp grated lemon rind
juice of 1 lemon
4 tbsp butter

Combine first five ingredients in a small saucepan, and set on the side of the grill. Let simmer about 10 minutes. Remove from the fire, and add the butter, a spoonful at a time, until it melts and sauce is slightly thickened. Use to baste chicken.

(Makes approximately 1 cup)

6 ◇ Meats

Whole Beef Fillet ◇ Boog's Burgers ◇ Bali Burgers ◇
Cajun-Style Ribs ◇ Korean Barbecued Short Ribs ◇ Easy
Barbecued Flank Steak ◇ Stuffed Flank Steak ◇ Round Steak in
Coffee Marinade ◇ Steak Gaucho ◇ Pepper Steak ◇ Korean
Barbecued Beef ◇ Thai Beef Strips ◇ Wine-Glazed Ham Steaks
◇ Classic Lamb Chops ◇ Lamb Chops in Mustard Sauce ◇
Grilled Lamb in Red Pepper Sauce ◇ Tandoori Lamb ◇
Barbecued Lamb Shanks ◇ Liver with Sage ◇ Beer-Barbecued
Pork Chops ◇ Pork Chops with Chili Sauce ◇ Pork
Sandwiches ◇ Inside-Out Ribs ◇ Mesquite-Smoked Ribs ◇
Canton-Style Ribs ◇ Pork in Mushroom-Wine Sauce ◇ New
Mexican-Style Soft-Shell Tacos ◇ Grilled Veal
Chops with Sage

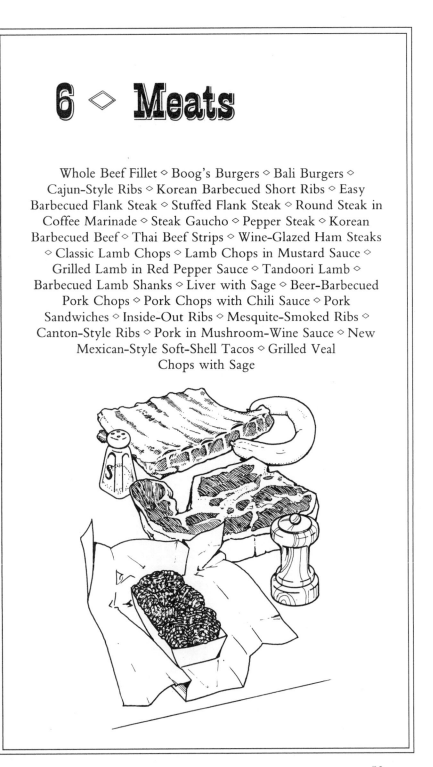

◇

When we think of the outdoor grill, usually the first thing that comes to mind is meat—all sorts of meat. Nothing brings out the subtle, juicy, sizzling flavor of meat better than a hot grill wrapped in the smoke of mesquite.

But in order to enjoy the delightful flavor imparted to meat by this cooking fuel, you must exercise a little know-how. Be extra careful: it's easy to overcook meat to the point of dryness, the archenemy of all outdoor cooking. However, meat cooked over mesquite will never be dry if you follow a few simple rules.

A good rule of thumb is that basic meat cuts—except for ribs and such—should range from 1 to 3 inches in thickness. It's also important to let meat reach room temperature before placing it on your grill. This makes for the most balanced flavor and juiciest results.

Another thing I've learned: Nick the border of fat around the steak at ½-inch intervals before placing it on the hot grill. By doing this you will be spared the embarrassment of serving one of those funny-looking "buckled-up" steaks.

Also, always sear the steak or other meat first, then let it cook according to the recipe's directions. With pork and lamb, it's best to baste them regularly with some plain oil to keep them moist.

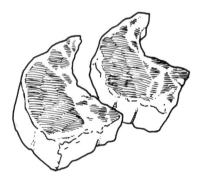

◇ Whole Beef Fillet

    1 5-lb. whole beef fillet
    ¼ cup peppercorns, crushed
    ⅓ cup cognac or brandy, warmed in a small pan and placed
       on grill

Sauce

    1 cup heavy cream
    2 tbsp French mustard
    1 tbsp Worcestershire sauce
    1 tbsp lemon juice

Press crushed peppercorns into the fillet. Grill over mesquite, turning once. Place meat thermometer into thickest part of fillet.

When the thermometer registers 120°F, the fillet is done. (*Note:* Although not always available, a meat thermometer can take the guessing out of the barbecuing for many dishes. I personally like to stick with the touch test method, which only comes with experience.) Brush off excess pepper, and immediately place meat on a heated platter. Pour cognac over the meat and flame.

Make sauce while the meat is cooking. Combine first three ingredients in a saucepan, and bring to a gentle boil, stirring constantly for 3 minutes to thicken slightly. Stir in lemon juice and remove from heat. Carve the fillet, making three thin slices for each serving. Add the juices from carving to the sauce, and pour the sauce over each serving.

(Serves 6 to 8)

◇ Boog's Burgers

    1 lb lean ground beef
    1 tsp parsley, finely chopped
    1 tsp fresh or dry thyme leaves, finely chopped
    2 to 3 slices bacon, fried and finely crumbled

Form beef into four equal patties. Mix parsley, thyme, and bacon bits together. In the center of each patty place one-quarter of the herb and bacon mixture. Thoroughly combine the mixture with the beef, to make patties approximately 1 inch thick. Grill burgers over hot mesquite for 4 to 6 minutes per side for rare and about 7 to 9 minutes for medium and well done.

Variations: Stuffed burgers can be made with your favorite herbs and fillings, so experiment. Other delicious combinations include ham and parsley; mushrooms and feta cheese; chopped parsley, garlic, and cumin.

(Serves 4)

◇ *Bali Burgers*

> *1 lb pork, finely ground*
> *1 lb beef, finely ground*
> *2 garlic cloves, crushed*
> *2 tbsp ground coriander*
> *1 tsp nutmeg, freshly grated if available*
> *½ cup green onions, chopped*
> *1 egg, lightly beaten*
> *salt and freshly ground pepper*
> *peanut oil*

Knead all ingredients except oil into meat, and shape into eight equal burger patties. Place burgers over hot mesquite coals. Brush with small amounts of peanut oil while cooking until nicely browned.

(Serves 8)

◇ *Cajun-Style Ribs*

¼ cup coarse salt
⅓ cup brown sugar
2 tbsp ground pepper
1 tbsp grated lemon rind
1 tbsp Tabasco sauce
2 tbsp paprika
5 lb beef ribs

Sauce

1 cup chicken or beef broth
⅓ cup Worcestershire sauce
½ cup vinegar
¼ cup corn oil
1 tsp mustard
1 tbsp chili powder
1 tbsp pepper
1 tsp cayenne pepper
1 tbsp white pepper
1 tbsp Tabasco sauce
1 garlic clove, crushed

Make a paste from the salt, brown sugar, pepper, lemon rind, Tabasco sauce, and paprika. Rub paste into ribs and marinate in refrigerator overnight. Cook ribs according to the directions on page 71, Canton-Style Ribs.

For sauce, mix all of the ingredients into a small saucepan and slowly bring to a boil. Baste the ribs about every 25 minutes. Baste ribs lightly just before serving.

(Serves 2 to 4)

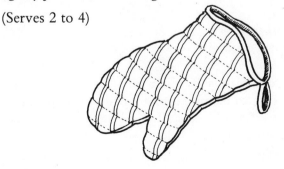

◇ *Korean Barbecued Short Ribs*

4 to 5 lb beef short ribs, 2½ inches long

Marinade

>*1 tbsp sesame seeds*
>*1 cup soy sauce*
>*2 tbsp Mirin (sweet rice wine) or sherry*
>*3 tbsp sugar*
>*2 tsp fresh ginger, finely minced*
>*4 garlic cloves, crushed*
>*2 tbsp dried red pepper, finely chopped*

Toast sesame seeds in pan over low flame. Grind sesame seeds in mortar and pestle and add to marinade. Place ribs in a large plastic bag. Combine marinade ingredients and pour over ribs, pressing air out of bag and sealing securely. Marinate in refrigerator at least 4 hours. Remove ribs from bag, shaking off excess marinade. Grill ribs over hot mesquite 15 to 25 minutes, turning and basting just before removing from the grill. Ribs are ready when brown and crispy.

(Serves 2 to 4)

◇ *Easy Barbecued Flank Steak*

>*2 lb beef flank steak*
>*1 garlic clove, crushed*
>*2 to 3 tbsp soy sauce*
>*1 tbsp tomato paste*
>*1 tbsp oil*
>*¼ tsp black pepper*
>*1 tbsp fresh oregano leaves*

Score the flank steak diagonally on both sides. In a blender mix remaining ingredients to a smooth paste, and pour over the steak. Marinate in the refrigerator overnight. Grill the steak over hot mesquite for 4 to 7 minutes on each side.

(Serves 4)

◇ *Stuffed Flank Steak*

4 lb flank steak

Marinade

salt and freshly ground pepper
1/4 *cup fresh parsley, finely chopped*
1 *medium onion, chopped*
1/4 *cup red wine vinegar*
1/4 *cup olive oil*

Filling

1 *cup chopped cooked spinach*
1 *cup fresh green peas*
2 *tbsp grated Parmesan cheese*
1 1/2 *cups bread cubes*
salt and freshly ground pepper
4 *slender carrots*
4 *small hard-cooked eggs*
6 *slices bacon*
1/4 *tsp ground nutmeg*

Combine marinade ingredients in a shallow baking dish. Allow the flank steak to marinate for 12 hours or overnight. Turn two or three times. Reserve marinade for basting.

In a large bowl combine spinach, peas, cheese, and bread. Add salt and pepper to taste.

Lay the steak flat and spread filling on top in a layer. Place carrots and eggs along the length of the steak, and top with bacon slices. Roll flank steak lengthwise and tie securely with string.

Place stuffed flank steak on spit. Roast for 1 1/2 to 2 hours. Meat should be placed 10 to 12 inches from mesquite. Brush with marinade periodically.

(Serves 6 to 8)

◇ *Round Steak in Coffee Marinade*

2 or 3 round steaks, 1¼ inches thick

Marinade

> *½ cup coffee*
> *1 6-ounce can frozen orange juice concentrate, defrosted*
> *2 tbsp minced onion*
> *1 tbsp salt*
> *1 tbsp lemon juice*
> *⅛ tsp cloves*
> *1 tbsp Tabasco sauce*

Combine marinade ingredients. Place steaks in marinade and refrigerate for 6 hours or overnight. Remove and let stand until they reach room temperature. Place steaks over mesquite coals, about 4 to 5 inches from heat. Broil for 20 to 25 minutes at moderate temperature. Turn occasionally and brush with marinade.

(Serves 4 to 6)

◇ *Steak Gaucho*

2 3-inch-thick sirloin steaks, approximately 3½ to 4 lb each

Sauce

> *½ lb butter*
> *2 cups scallions or 1½ cups onions, finely chopped*
> *½ tsp dried rosemary, crumbled*
> *½ tsp oregano leaves, crumbled*
> *1 cup dry white wine*
> *½ cup wine vinegar or cider vinegar*
> *1½ tsp salt*
> *1 tbsp freshly ground black pepper*
> *2 tbsp butter*

Sauté chopped scallions or onions in butter about 10 minutes over medium heat until limp but not brown. Add rosemary, oregano, wine, vinegar, salt, and pepper. Remove from heat, season to taste, and add remaining 2 tablespoons of butter. Reserve sauce for later use. Broil steaks over hot mesquite coals approximately 15 minutes on each side for rare steaks. Just before serving, warm sauce on low heat, carve steak, and pour sauce over steak slices.

(Serves 6)

◇ *Pepper Steak*

6 8–12 oz *top sirloin steaks*
3 tbsp black peppercorns, coarsely ground
1/4 cup cognac, warmed
salt

Pat steaks dry with paper towels. Using the palm of your hand, gently but firmly press crushed peppercorns into both sides of the meat. Grill steaks over hot mesquite coals until browned on both sides. Pour warm cognac over steaks and ignite. The flame will burn for only a few minutes. Once the flame goes out, quickly scrape off excess pepper, salt to taste, and serve.

(Serves 6)

◇ *Korean Barbecued Beef*

2 lb sirloin, rib, or flank steak

Marinade

3 scallions, finely chopped
4 garlic cloves, crushed
5 tbsp soy sauce
2 tbsp sesame oil
1 tbsp sesame seeds
1/4 cup sugar
2 tbsp sherry or mirin (sweet rice wine)
1/8 tsp black pepper

Slice the steak diagonally against the grain into very thin strips. Score each piece lightly. (This prevents meat from curling as it is barbecuing.) Combing remaining ingredients in bowl, mix well, then add meat. Allow to marinate for several hours or overnight.

To prevent overcooking, grill meat just until it turns color, then remove from heat. Remember, all meats continue to cook even when taken off heat. Serve with white rice.

(Serves 6)

◇ *Thai Beef Strips*

1/2 cup soy sauce
1/4 cup sugar
 6 garlic cloves, finely chopped
 2 tbsp sesame seeds, toasted
1/4 cup thinly sliced scallions
1/4 cup fresh coriander leaves, finely chopped
 1 tablespoon fresh ginger, minced
 2 lb boneless lean beef, thinly sliced

Dipping Sauce

1/3 cup sugar
 2 tbsp cornstarch
1/3 cup soy sauce
 3 tbsp vinegar
3/4 tsp crushed dried red pepper

Combine first seven ingredients to make a marinade. Then add beef strips, cover, and let stand in refrigerator at least 2 hours before grilling. This marinade can be made ahead of time and stored in refrigerator.

To make the dipping sauce, combine sugar and cornstarch in a saucepan. Add the soy sauce, vinegar, and crushed red pepper. Stir all ingredients over low heat. Continue stirring and increase heat slightly until mixture begins to bubble and thicken. Place in a shallow bowl and set aside.

Grill beef strips on a barbeque, taking care not to overcook. On a mesquite grill this should take only about ½ minute per side of each strip. Serve with sauce.

(Serves 6)

◇ *Wine-Glazed Ham Steaks*

1 lb center-cut ham slice, 1 in thick

Sauce

½ cup dry white wine
¼ cup orange juice
¼ cup maple syrup
1 tbsp cornstarch, dissolved in 2 tsp white wine vinegar
½ tsp dry mustard
¼ tsp ground ginger

Combine all ingredients except ham in saucepan. Bring the sauce to a slow boil, stirring constantly, then reduce heat and simmer for a few minutes. Grill ham over mesquite coals. Brush frequently with sauce on both sides, allowing 10 minutes of cooking time for each side. When done, place ham on serving dish, and pour remaining sauce over entire dish.

(Serves 4)

◇ *Classic Lamb Chops*

6 baby loin lamb chops, 1½ inches thick

Marinade

½ *cup tomato sauce*
⅓ *cup red wine*
¼ *cup olive oil*
1 *tsp fresh lime or lemon juice*
1 *cup chopped onion*
1 *garlic clove, crushed*
1 *tbsp chili powder*
1 *tsp salt*
½ *tsp dried thyme*
½ *tsp ground cumin*
½ *tsp dried oregano*

Combine marinade ingredients, and marinate chops for at least 4 hours. (If you prepare marinade the night before serving, the results will be even tastier). Cook the chops for approximately 8 to 10 minutes on each side, basting with marinade while cooking.

(Serves 4 to 6)

◇ *Lamb Chops in Mustard Sauce*

4 lamb chops, 2 to 3 inches thick
2 garlic cloves, crushed
2 tbsp lemon juice
6 tbsp olive oil
salt and pepper

Mustard Butter

4 tbsp butter
1 tbsp Dijon mustard
1 garlic clove, crushed
½ *tsp lemon juice*
1 tsp tarragon

Rub the lamb chops with the crushed garlic. Then gently apply the lemon juice. Finally, brush the lamb chops with the olive oil and season with salt and pepper. Let the chops marinate at least 2 to 3 hours.

To make the mustard butter, bring the butter to room temperature and add the remaining ingredients.

The secret to perfect and succulent lamb chops is the proper thickness of chop and the fast searing that mesquite cooking affords. Cook the chops over the hottest part of the grill for 3 to 4 minutes on each side. Then, move chops to a moderately hot part of the grill and grill for about 3 to 4 minutes per side to ensure the slow cooking that preserves the chops' tender juiciness. Serve the chops with a dollop of mustard butter.

(Serves 4)

◇ *Grilled Lamb in Red Pepper Sauce*

> *2 red peppers*
> *2 medium shallots*
> *⅛ cup red wine vinegar*
> *2 tbsp olive oil*
> *2 1½-inch-thick lamb chops*

Roast red peppers over mesquite, turning often. When flesh is tender, remove charred skin, split pepper, and remove the seeds and veins. In a small pan sauté shallots in olive oil over a low flame until brown. Place red pepper, olive oil, and shallots in blender. Add red wine vinegar to the same pan and return to low flame. After just a few minutes deglaze pan with a wooden spoon. Add vinegar to blender and puree. Set aside until ready to serve.

Grill lamb chops over a medium low mesquite fire, turning once or twice. They should be done when the meat close to the bone is just slightly pink and the outside is crispy and brown—about 9 to 12 minutes. At serving time, warm puree and pour over chops.

(Serves 2)

◇ *Tandoori Lamb*

> *2 lb lamb chops, cubed*

> *Marinade*

> *Same as for Indian Yogurt Marinade (page 39)*

> *Relish*

>> *1 cup yogurt*
>> *3 tbsp fresh mint, finely chopped*
>> *1½ cucumbers, finely diced*
>> *2 fresh tomatoes, chopped*

Cut lamb chops into 1-inch cubes and place them in a bowl. Prepare marinade. Marinate lamb overnight in refrigerator. Remove meat from refrigerator about 1 hour before grilling. Skewer pieces of lamb and grill them over low fire for 8 to 10 minutes, depending on desired doneness. In a bowl, toss yogurt, chopped mint leaves, cucumbers, and tomatoes. Chill this relish for half an hour before serving. Serve large dollops of relish as an accompaniment to sizzling lamb skewers.

(Serves 4)

◇ *Barbecued Lamb Shanks*

> *6 lamb shanks*

> *Marinade*

>> *1 cup oil*
>> *1 cup dry vermouth*
>> *1 tbsp fresh lemon juice*
>> *3 shallots or 1 medium-sized onion, chopped*
>> *2 garlic cloves, finely chopped*
>> *1 tbsp chopped fresh or dry tarragon leaves*
>> *1 tbsp chopped fresh or dry basil leaves*
>> *1 tbsp salt*
>> *10 peppercorns, crushed*

Combine marinade ingredients in a glass jar, and shake vigorously to make a smooth marinade. Add to lamb shanks and let stand at room temperature for at least 4 hours. Turn lamb shanks in marinade every 30 minutes or so. Broil shanks over hot mesquite for about 30 minutes. Turn shanks every 10 minutes, basting with marinade on each side.

(Serves 4)

◇ *Liver with Sage*

1½ lb calf or beef liver, cut into 1½-in cubes
salt and freshly ground pepper
  2 tbsp chopped fresh sage
  1 tsp crumbled dried rosemary or 2 sprigs rosemary, chopped
juice of ½ lemon
olive oil
  6 slices bacon
  12 fresh sage leaves

Put liver in shallow dish. Sprinkle with salt and pepper, chopped sage, rosemary, and lemon juice. Drizzle with a little oil. Marinate 1 hour, turning occasionally. Wrap bacon around cubes and place on skewers, stuffing sage leaves between cubes. Grill over mesquite, brushing with marinade, until browned outside but still pink inside.

(Serves 4 to 6)

◇ *Beer-Barbecued Pork Chops*

8 loin pork chops, about 1¼ in thick

Sauce

¼ *cup cider vinegar*
¼ *cup Worcestershire sauce*
¼ *cup unsalted butter*
 1 medium onion, chopped
 1 tbsp celery seed
 2 garlic cloves, finely minced
 1 tsp dry mustard
 1 tsp granulated sugar
 1 tsp salt
 1 tsp cayenne or freshly ground black pepper
 1 14-ounce bottle ketchup
 1 cup flat Miller Lite Beer

Combine sauce ingredients in a 2-quart saucepan. Simmer uncovered over medium heat for 15 minutes, stirring frequently to maintain a smooth sauce. Set aside for later use. (Makes approximately 3 cups sauce.)

After attaining a very hot fire, place chops on the grill and sear meat for about 5 minutes on each side. Remove chops from grill, cover grill with heavy-duty aluminum foil, then poke holes into foil for ventilation. Again, place chops onto grill and spoon generous amounts of sauce over chops. Cook for 10 minutes on one side, then turn chops over, placing generous amounts of sauce on second side. Continue turning chops approximately every 5 minutes, adding sauce until chops are thoroughly cooked, about 30 minutes. The meat is done when the inside is white. You can check by cutting through to the bone of a chop.

(Serves 4)

◇ *Pork Chops with Chili Sauce*

8 pork chops, 1 in thick

Marinade

3 tbsp chili powder
3 tbsp tomato juice
4 garlic cloves, crushed
1 tsp salt
1/3 tsp dried oregano leaves

Cold Green Chili Sauce

1/4 cup fresh green chilies, finely chopped
2 canned jalapeño chilies, finely chopped
3 tomatoes, peeled, seeded, and finely chopped
1/2 cup chopped scallions
1 garlic clove, crushed
2 tbsp fresh parsley, finely chopped
1 tsp dried coriander, soaked in 1 tbsp hot water and drained
1/2 tsp salt
pinch black pepper
pinch sugar

Combine marinade ingredients into a paste, and spread over both sides of the chops. Cover the chops and marinate them overnight in the refrigerator.

Combine all of the sauce ingredients and refrigerate for at least 1 hour to chill thoroughly.

Remove excess fat from chops and grill over hot mesquite until tender and browned—about 15 minutes. Serve the chops with the cold chili sauce.

(Serves 4)

◇ *Pork Sandwiches*

>   2 lb pork loin, in 1-in-thick slices
>   ½ cup white vinegar
>   1 to 2 tsp hot red pepper, crushed
>   1 onion, chopped
>   2 garlic cloves, crushed
>   olive oil
>   crushed rosemary
>   crusty round rolls or hamburger buns
>   salt and freshly ground pepper to taste

Marinate pork in a mixture of vinegar, red pepper, onion, and garlic for 1 hour at room temperature. Pat the pork steaks dry and rub them with olive oil. Sprinkle pork steaks with crushed rosemary. Grill about 5 to 7 minutes on each side over hot mesquite. Serve on lightly buttered rolls or buns toasted on the grill. Season with salt and pepper to taste.

(Serves 6)

◇ *Inside-Out Ribs*

>   4 to 5 lb pork ribs
>   6 bay leaves
>   1 tsp white pepper
>   3 tbsp crushed peppercorns
>   1 large head garlic, peeled and quartered
>   1 tbsp crushed fresh ginger (optional)
>   ½ cup fresh orange juice
>   2 qt tomato juice

Parboil ribs for 10 to 15 minutes in a large pan of boiling water. Drain and set aside. In a roasting pan combine all the remaining ingredients. Add the ribs, cover with an aluminum foil tent, and bake in a 350°F oven until tender (2 to 2½ hours). Remove the ribs from the sauce and set aside. Cook the remaining sauce until it reduces into a thick ketchuplike consistency. Discard bay leaves.

When sauce is ready place ribs over a moderately hot mesquite grill for about 30 minutes. Baste the ribs every 5 minutes.

Warm the remaining sauce and serve with the ribs hot from the grill.

(Serves 3 to 4)

◇ *Mesquite-Smoked Ribs*

4 to 5 lb pork ribs
5 bay leaves
2 tsp salt
3 tbsp peppercorns, crushed
1 tsp chili powder

Parboil ribs in boiling water for 10 to 15 minutes; drain. Combine all remaining ingredients in a large roasting pan. Place ribs in pan with sauce and bake in preheated oven until tender (about 2 hours, 350°F). Remove ribs from pan and reduce the remaining sauce over a low flame until it turns into a syruplike consistency.

At serving time, grill ribs over mesquite at a medium low heat in a covered barbecue. Turn and baste often for 20 to 30 minutes.

(Serves 3 to 4)

◇ *Canton-Style Ribs*

4 to 5 lb lean pork spareribs
1/4 cup sugar
1 tbsp rice wine or dry sherry
1/4 cup hoisin sauce
1 tbsp oyster sauce
1/2 tsp five-spice powder
1/2 tsp saltpeter (optional; gives pork the red color)

Cut spareribs in half lengthwise to make approximately two even pieces. Mix remaining ingredients until smooth, rub marinade over both slabs of spareribs, and marinate for at least 4 hours at room temperature. Place on mesquite grill, being careful not to burn ribs by turning occasionally. Ribs cook in about 45 minutes to 1 hour.

(Serves 3 to 4)

◇ *Pork in Mushroom-Wine Sauce*

> 1 lb pork tenderloin, cut into ¼-inch slices
> ¼ cup olive oil
> 1 tsp fresh rosemary, minced
> 2 garlic cloves, minced or crushed
> 2 cups mushrooms
> 3½ tbsp butter
> 2 cups madeira or other sweet red wine
> salt and pepper

Mix the olive oil, rosemary, and garlic in a stainless steel or glass bowl. Marinate the pork slices in this mixture, covered, for 3 to 4 hours in the refrigerator. In a saucepan, sauté the mushrooms until limp in 2 tablespoons of the butter. Add the wine and reduce the mixture to approximately 1 cup while stirring constantly over high heat. Whisk in the remaining 1½ tablespoons of butter and season to taste. Keep warm until ready to serve.

Grill the pork slices over a hot mesquite fire. When you see drops of blood surfacing on the side away from the fire, turn immediately and cook for approximately the same amount of time on the other side. This is a very fast procedure, probably taking no more than 3 or 4 minutes. Serve the pork slices on hot plates and ladle on the mushroom sauce.

(Serves 4)

◇ *New Mexican-Style Soft-Shell Tacos*

> 1½ lb pork (tenderloin, shoulder chops, or roast)

Sauce

> 16 to 18 dried red chilies
> 2 garlic cloves
> 2 tsp salt
> 3 garlic cloves, crushed
> 1 tsp dried oregano
> 12 tortillas

First prepare red chili sauce. Open each red chili pod, wash, and remove stems, seeds, and veins. (For hotter sauce leave some veins.) Soak the pods in hot water until soft (about 1 hour). Place the pods in a blender or food processor, adding just enough water to cover. Blend until smooth, adding 2 garlic cloves near the end of blending. If too thick, add a little more water to reach desired consistency. Add salt, crushed garlic, and oregano to chili sauce. Slice the pork into thin, flat pieces, then flatten pieces with a meat cleaver as much as possible. Pour chili sauce marinade over pork and refrigerate overnight.

Grill pork over medium flame for just a few minutes, turning often. In the meantime, heat tortillas over grill, turning often. As the tortillas are heated, wrap them in a clean towel to keep them hot and stack them next to the grill. Take the meat from the grill, dice it, wrap it in the tortillas, and serve. This dish is best accompanied by a spicy chili salsa (see page 67).

(Serves 4)

◇ *Grilled Veal Chops with Sage*

> 6 veal rib chops, 1 in thick
> 1 cup olive oil
> ¼ cup fresh sage, chopped
> 4 garlic cloves, crushed
> salt
> freshly ground pepper

Whisk oil, sage, and garlic in small bowl until blended; pour over veal chops in shallow baking dish. Turn chops to coat evenly, then let marinate, covered, at room temperature up to 4 hours or in refrigerator up to 2 days.

Prepare mesquite fire in barbecue. When fire is ready, lift chops from marinade, setting marinade aside. Pat chops with paper towel to remove excess marinade; season with salt and pepper. Grill chops 4 to 5 minutes per side for medium rare. Brush with reserved marinade before serving.

(Serves 6)

7 ◇ Poultry

Grilled Chicken with Asparagus ◇ Smoky Beer Chicken ◇
Chicken Diablo ◇ Japanese Lemon Chicken ◇ Grilled Chicken
with Mole Sauce ◇ Sweet and Sour Chicken ◇ Tex-Mex
Chicken ◇ Thai-Style Chicken ◇ Chicken in Barbecued
Vegetable Sauce ◇ Barbecued Chicken Wings ◇ Cajun-Style
Duck ◇ Lemon Duck ◇ Spicy Game Hen ◇ Orioles in Garlic ◇
Roast Turkey with Pomegranates ◇ Texas Turkey

◇

The poultry family has always been a favorite for the outdoor grill. One of the reasons for that is because poultry flesh, if cooked right, is deliciously tender. With mesquite, every variety of poultry—from turkey to duck and chicken—surpasses itself in flavor when cooked in this fashion over the outdoor grill. The skin especially seems to absorb the mesquite aroma and crisps beautifully.

For best results put in a little extra work here. Of all the items that go over the grill, only fish and shellfish need basting as often as poultry does.

Chicken is perhaps the most durable of outdoor main dishes. In this section the recipes demonstrate a wide variety of mesquite techniques, from the mild smoked chicken in the Smoky Beer Chicken recipe to the more ambitious Grilled Chicken with Mole Sauce, a recipe created over 500 years ago by the ancient Aztec.

In order to become a pro in outdoor grilling with poultry you will have to master one technique. The trick is to cook up a skin that is crunchy crisp while keeping the meat inside tender and juicy. Follow the recipes I've provided, and you're on your way.

◇ Grilled Chicken with Asparagus

> 1 2-lb chicken, halved
> 1½ lb large asparagus, parboiled in water for 5 minutes
> ¼ cup fresh lemon juice
> ¼ cup butter, melted
> salt and pepper

Grill chicken halves over hot mesquite fire for 4 to 6 minutes on each side. Two minutes before chicken is done, move it to a spot on the grill where fire is not too hot. Place the asparagus where the chicken was originally. Cook the asparagus 1½ to 2½ minutes, depending on the size of the fire. Remove the cooked asparagus to a large serving plate. Next, remove the chicken halves, placing them on a bed of asparagus. Pour lemon juice and butter over the platter and serve. Salt and pepper to taste.

(Serves 4)

◇ Smoky Beer Chicken

> 1 4-lb chicken, quartered

Sauce

> 1 cup tomato sauce
> 1 tbsp soy sauce
> 2 tbsp white vinegar
> ¾ cup flat Miller Lite Beer (tough to find in my house)
> 1 tsp salt
> 1 tsp dried red chilies, crushed
> 1 tsp black pepper
> 1 garlic clove, crushed

> aluminum foil
> presoaked hickory chips

Precook chicken in preheated 400°F oven for about 20 to 25 minutes. Reserve some chicken drippings for your sauce. Combine remaining ingredients in a saucepan and simmer uncovered for 15 to 20 minutes. Remove the grill from the fire while the mesquite is heating, wrap the grill carefully with foil, and punch holes in foil for air circulation. If you don't have a barbecue with a lid, make a foil tent for the grill. Make sure to punch several small holes in tent. Once the mesquite is ready, put presoaked hickory chips on the fire. Smoke chicken on grill for about 1 hour, turning and basting often with the sauce.

(Serves 4)

◇ Chicken Diablo

3 to 4 lbs of chicken, cut-up

Marinade

½ cup olive or peanut oil
juice of 1 lemon or 3 tbsp lemon juice
2 tbsp Dijon mustard
4 dashes Tabasco or liquid chili pepper sauce

Clean chicken parts, pat dry, and set aside until pieces reach room temperature. Mix remaining ingredients to make a marinade. Set aside. About 30 minutes before grilling, coat chicken pieces thoroughly with marinade. Cook over a moderate mesquite fire, skin-side down. In order to avoid flare-up, you may want to remove skins before grilling. Grill about 15 minutes on each side. Baste chicken with marinade while cooking.

(Serves 4)

◇ Japanese Lemon Chicken

1 fat broiler chicken, quartered (about 3 lb)
salt
2 lemons
1 1-in piece fresh gingerroot, peeled and sliced
2 tbsp soy sauce
2 tbsp rice wine
1 tbsp sesame oil

78

¼ cup peanut oil
4 garlic cloves, crushed
20 to 30 sprigs chopped fresh cilantro

Wash chicken and pat dry. Sprinkle with salt and let stand 30 minutes. Grate the peel and squeeze the juice of 1 lemon into a bowl with the rest of the ingredients; reserve 1 lemon and some cilantro. Marinate chicken in mixture at room temperature 2 hours or more; turn occasionally to ensure chicken has marinated fully. Grill chicken over mesquite coals about 20 minutes or until nicely browned. Turn chicken occasionally and brush with marinade. Place chicken in serving dish and pour remaining marinade over grilled chicken. Thinly slice remaining lemon and garnish chicken with lemon slices and cilantro.

(Serves 4)

◇ Grilled Chicken with Mole Sauce

4 chicken breasts, skinned (optional)
⅛ cup olive oil
2 tbsp chili powder

Mole Sauce

½ cup pumpkin seeds
6 poblano chili peppers
1 tbsp peanut butter
1 cup warm chicken broth
1 tsp salt
fresh ground pepper to taste
4 tbsp chopped cilantro
1 garlic clove, halved

Bone chicken breast. Place chicken pieces between waxed paper and pound until thin. Mix olive oil and chili powder and coat chicken with this mixture. Marinate for 1 hour before cooking. Cook over medium hot flame for only a minute or two or just until all the flesh turns white in color.

To make mole sauce toast the pumpkin seeds until brown and crisp. Place chilies over open flame or in oven until skins blister and can easily be removed by hand. Remove the core and seeds from chilies. In a blender, mix the seeds and chilies into a paste. Add peanut butter and warm chicken broth, and blend again. Warm mixture in a small saucepan over a low flame. Add salt, pepper, cilantro, and the garlic clove. At serving time pour mole sauce over hot grilled chicken.

(Serves 4)

◇ *Sweet and Sour Chicken*

3 to 4 lb chicken, cut up

Sauce

¾ cup ketchup
¾ cup apricot preserves
2 tbsp white or cider vinegar
1 tsp Worcestershire sauce
1 tbsp mild chili powder
½ tsp salt

Combine sauce ingredients in a 2-quart saucepan. Stir occasionally over medium heat until sauce starts to boil. Reduce heat to simmer. Allow mixture to cook for 5 minutes, uncovered. Set the sauce aside to cool. Marinate the chicken for 1 to 2 hours.

Place grilling rack 4 to 5 inches from mesquite coals. Grill chicken skin-side up for 20 minutes, then baste and turn about every 5 minutes until chicken is done. Chicken may be served with sauce on the side or in shallow baking dish with sauce poured on top.

(Serves 3)

◇ Tex-Mex Chicken

1 3- to 4-lb chicken, halved, with backbone removed
1 lemon, halved

Marinade

6 garlic cloves, crushed
1 tbsp cayenne pepper
1 tbsp white pepper
2 tbsp paprika
salt

Wash chicken thoroughly. Pat dry. Rub both sides with half a lemon. In a small bowl mix garlic and spices. Rub mixture on both sides of chicken. Place the chicken halves, skin-side up, in a shallow baking dish. Allow the chicken to stand covered in refrigerator for 24 hours. Place the chicken halves, skin-side up, 4–5 inches from mesquite coals. Cover and grill for 20 minutes, turn and grill at 20- to 30-minute intervals. Total cooking time is about 1½ hours.

(Serves 4)

◇ Thai-Style Chicken

1 2- to 3-lb frying chicken, quartered

Marinade

½ cup soy sauce
½ cup sherry or Mirin (sweet rice wine)
1 tbsp grated fresh gingerroot or 1 tsp dried ginger
1 garlic clove, minced
1 tbsp sesame oil
4 tbsp cilantro, finely chopped

Thoroughly mix all the marinade ingredients in a large bowl. Marinate chicken for about 1 hour. Grill skin-side up, turning at the end of broiling so that the skin sears and finally crisps. From time to time baste chicken while grilling. Depending on size, chicken takes anywhere from 20 to 35 minutes to cook.

(Serves 3 to 4)

◇ *Chicken in Barbecued Vegetable Sauce*

4 to 6 chicken breasts with bone
lemon wedges

Sauce

2 onions
2 green bell peppers
2 fresh serrano chilies
6 tomatoes
½ lb smoked ham
salt
pepper
sugar
6 each, green and black pitted olives, halved

Grill vegetables whole on mesquite grill until charred on the outside, then place them in a paper bag and close tightly, letting them cool until able to be handled. Remove from bag and peel skins. Cut smoked ham into chunks, skewer, and roast on grill until charred. Remove the skins from the vegetables. Chop up chilies, removing the veins, seeds, and stems. Chop up onions and tomatoes, and put all the vegetables in a saucepan with the charred smoked ham. Add seasonings and olives. Simmer sauce uncovered until thick.

Brush chicken liberally while grilling. Serve the chicken topped off with the remaining vegetable sauce. Garnish with lemon wedges.

(Serves 4 to 6)

◇ *Barbecued Chicken Wings*

12 chicken wings
½ cup honey, melted

Marinade

¼ cup olive oil
1 lemon
2 garlic cloves, crushed
1 1-in piece fresh gingerroot, grated
salt and pepper

Remove chicken wing tips and break wings into two pieces. Combine marinade ingredients and marinate the wings for 2 hours. Place wings on grill over medium fire for 3 to 4 minutes on each side, turning continually. To finish wings with a sweet, crispy flavor, brush wings with honey while they're still on the grill. Careful turning is required to prevent the skin from burning.

(Serves 2)

◇ *Cajun-Style Duck with Roasted Pepper Mayonnaise*

2 duck breasts (about 1 lb total), skinned, boned, halved,
   and lightly pounded
½ cup dry red wine

Roasted Pepper Mayonnaise

 2 red bell peppers
 2 egg yolks
 1 tbsp wine vinegar
juice of ½ lemon
 ½ tsp soy sauce
 1 tsp ground white pepper
1½ tsp Dijon mustard
 1 cup vegetable oil
dash Tabasco sauce
 1 shallot, finely minced
 1 tbsp boiling water

Place duck in a large bowl, add wine, cover, and allow to stand for 3 hours.

To prepare mayonnaise, cook whole peppers in boiling water for 2 minutes and drain. Place peppers on mesquite grill, cook for 15 minutes, turn, and cook for 10 to 15 minutes until both sides are soft and charred. Peel the peppers using knife; remove ribs, stem, and seeds. Dice finely and reserve. In a large bowl beat egg yolks until light. Continue beating and slowly add vinegar, lemon juice, soy sauce, white pepper, and mustard. Beat in oil, 1 tablespoon at a time, until mixture thickens. Add Tabasco sauce, shallot, boiling water, and peppers. Refrigerate.

Drain duck breasts and place on grill, skin-side up, 4 to 5 inches from coals. Turn breasts after 10 minutes, then turn every 5 minutes, basting as you turn. Cook until tender, approximately 25 to 30 minutes. When fully cooked, serve on platter and spoon on remaining mayonnaise.

(Serves 2)

◇ *Lemon Duck*

1 4-lb duck, quartered

Sauce

4 green onions, chopped
1 tsp gingerroot, grated, or dried ginger
2 tsp turmeric
2 tbsp soy sauce
1 tsp sugar
1/2 tsp lemon peel, grated
salt
pepper

Combine all sauce ingredients and let duck marinate for about 4 hours. Turn occasionally to get even flavoring.

Grill duck over a roasting pan ringed with mesquite for 18 to 22 minutes per side or until skin is crisp. Water and a little lemon juice in roasting pan will help keep duck moist and lemony.

(Serves 4)

◇ *Spicy Game Hen*

4 game hens
1/2 cup soy sauce
2 garlic cloves
1/2 tsp fresh gingerroot, minced, or powdered ginger
2 tbsp honey

Dip

3 tbsp orange rind
1 tsp curry powder
1 tsp finely diced serrano chili pepper (if not available, use 1/4 tsp dried red peppers, crushed)
2 tbsp sesame oil
3 tbsp soy sauce
1 tbsp sherry or Mirin (sweet rice wine)
1/3 tsp cinnamon

Place soy sauce, garlic cloves, ginger, and honey in a blender. Pour over hens and marinate overnight. Make sure skins are coated with marinade.

Place hens skin-side up over hot mesquite grill. Cover with aluminum foil or lid and baste every 15 minutes with remaining marinade. Cook for 45 minutes in this manner. Then, turn hens skin-side down on grill. Cook for 15 minutes or long enough to crisp the skin.

Combine all dip ingredients except serrano chili pepper in a small bowl and mix thoroughly. Fifteen minutes before serving the dip, add the diced serrano chili pepper to taste. When serving the hen, serve the dip in small bowls to each guest.

(Serves 6 to 8)

◇ *Orioles in Garlic*

4 small squabs, game hens, or chickens
¼ lb butter
40 unpeeled cloves garlic
1 cup chicken stock
2 tbsp cognac
salt and freshly ground pepper
French or sourdough bread

Split birds in half and lightly rub with some butter. Place birds on grill for 20 to 25 minutes or until tender. Catch drippings in a drip pan.

Meanwhile, place garlic in a saucepan with the remaining butter and chicken stock, set on side of grill, covered, and allow to simmer. When the garlic is tender, set aside 12 cloves and put the rest of the cloves through a sieve into the butter broth. Add the drippings and cognac, and season to taste with salt and pepper. Serve birds on bread that has been toasted on the grill. Spoon sauce and reserved cloves of garlic over birds.

(Serves 4)

◇ Roast Turkey with Pomegranates

   1 8-lb turkey with giblets
   salt and freshly ground pepper
   1/2 cup butter
   6 slices bacon
   1/4 cup olive oil
   1 tsp ground cumin
   3 garlic cloves, minced
   3 pomegranates

Remove giblets and rub turkey cavity with salt, pepper, and butter. Truss openings. Skewer bacon securely over breast. Place turkey on spit and cook over mesquite coals for 1 hour. Baste. Continue to cook turkey for 1 hour or until tender. In a small saucepan, place chopped giblets, olive oil, cumin, and chopped garlic. Cook over medium heat until brown. Add juice and seeds of pomegranates and heat just until boiling. Serve the turkey with this spicy sauce on the side.

(Serves 6)

◇ Texas Turkey

   1 8-lb turkey, cut into 8 serving pieces

Sauce

1/4 cup vinegar
1/4 cup peanut oil
   1 tbsp strained fresh lemon juice
1/2 cup finely chopped onion
1/2 cup finely chopped green pepper
   1 tsp celery salt
1/4 tsp dried oregano
1/2 tsp dried basil
1/2 tsp white pepper
1/4 tsp ground cinnamon
1/4 tsp ground cumin
   1 garlic clove, crushed
   3 tbsp Tabasco sauce

In a small saucepan combine all ingredients except turkey and Tabasco. Cook over medium heat until onion is translucent. Remove the sauce from heat and allow it to cool. Add Tabasco to taste. Place the turkey pieces in shallow pan or bowl and marinate for several hours or overnight, turning occasionally. Before grilling, remove and drain turkey, reserve marinade. Turkey should be placed 4 to 5 inches from mesquite coals. Cook for 20 to 30 minutes on each side, basting as you turn.

(Serves 8)

8 ◇ Fish

Grilled Fish in Spicy Beer Sauce ◇ Crispy Grilled Fish ◇
Stuffed Fish with Avocado Sauce ◇ Barbecued Halibut ◇
Marinated Grilled Salmon ◇ Sea Bass Steak ◇ Grilled Whole
Sea Bass with Fresh Herbs ◇ Shark Steak with Chili Butter ◇
Classic Swordfish ◇ Grilled Trout ◇ Grilled Tuna with
Spiced Butter

◇

No other dish benefits as much from mesquite as does fish. There may be other fuels that will give heat equal to that of a mesquite fire, but there are none that allow mesquite's subtle flavor to be absorbed with such great effect as do the creatures of the sea.

The different varieties of fish seem to be the perfect foil for those who, like myself, have come to appreciate the aromatic accent of mesquite. But before you hurry to throw fish over the mesquite-fired grill, a word of caution is in order.

With fish, as with poultry, special care must be given to prevent dryness. Unlike many types of meats and poultry that require a high, intense flame, fish cooks best over mesquite that is medium-hot only. A good rule of thumb: always brush fish lightly with a coating of oil just before placing on the grill.

Salmon and tuna have more fat content than other types of fish and are the easiest to grill. Most other fish, such as sole, flounder, trout, or red snapper, require extra vigilance while you're cooking; they can be grilled in as little as 3 minutes on each side.

◇ Grilled Fish in Spicy Beer Sauce

3 to 4 pounds red snapper fillets

Sauce

> 2 ¼-inch-thick slices of slab bacon, cut into narrow strips
> and diced
> 2 medium onions, finely chopped
> 3 large garlic cloves, minced
> 16 oz tomato sauce
> 6 tbsp brown sugar, packed
> ¼ cup white wine vinegar
> 4 tbsp plus 2 tsp fresh lemon juice
> 10 oz flat Miller Lite Beer
> 1 tbsp Worcestershire sauce
> 1½ tbsp soy sauce
> 1 tsp each ground ginger, ground allspice, freshly ground
> nutmeg, and celery seed
> ½ teaspoon cayenne pepper
> salt to taste

In a small skillet sauté the bacon over medium flame until done lightly. Add onions and garlic and cook until translucent. Transfer mixture to a 2-quart saucepan. Add all remaining ingredients except salt. Bring sauce to a boil over medium heat. Simmer uncovered for 30 minutes, stirring occasionally. Remove from heat and allow sauce to cool. Salt to taste.

Place fish on grill about 3 inches from mesquite coals. Baste fish with sauce occasionally. Grill fish 3 to 4 minutes on each side, or a few minutes longer depending upon the thickness of fillets. Serve grilled fish on platter and spoon sauce over the fillets.

(Serves 4 to 6)

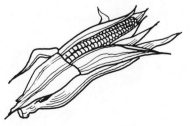

◇ *Crispy Grilled Fish*

1 3-lb whole fish (e.g., striped bass or red snapper)
4 tbsp clarified butter

Marinade

¼ cup coriander seeds
½ tsp paprika
1 onion, minced
2 garlic cloves, finely chopped
1 green pepper, finely chopped
6 whole cardamoms, pods removed and seeds separated
1 tbsp anise
¼ cup fresh parsley, finely chopped
2 tbsp fresh mint leaves, finely chopped
½ tsp salt
¼ tsp black pepper, freshly ground
⅔ cup yogurt
3 tbsp lemon or lime juice

Roast coriander seeds and paprika lightly in a frying pan. Mix in onions, garlic, green pepper, cardamoms, anise, parsley, mint, salt, and pepper to make a paste. Blend this mixture in a blender with yogurt and lemon or lime juice. Rub the paste all over the fish, including the internal cavity. Then marinate the fish in paste for 1 hour.

Place fish in a fish rack about 3 to 4 inches from a medium-hot mesquite fire. Grill the fish until the paste dries. This takes approximately 8 to 10 minutes for each side. Prevent the paste coat from burning by turning the fish, if necessary. Spread the mesquite coals farther apart to reduce the heat, and baste fish with butter and drippings. Repeat this procedure until fish flakes easily when pierced with a fork. To crisp the fish skin, use tongs to place the mesquite coals close together again. This increases the heat. Crisp for 2 to 3 minutes and serve.

(Serves 4)

◇ *Stuffed Fish With Avocado Sauce*

1 whole cleaned fish, approximately 3 lb (red snapper or sea bass)

Stuffing

1 garlic clove, minced
2 tbsp onions, finely chopped
¼ cup bread crumbs, finely crushed
1 tbsp minced parsley
salt
1 tsp hot red pepper, crushed
1 tsp dried thyme, crushed
¼ tsp nutmeg, freshly grated
2 tbsp fresh lemon juice
3 slices lemon

Sauce

2 large ripe avocados
3 tbsp lime juice
1 tbsp onion, finely grated
1 tsp salt
½ tsp black pepper, freshly ground
3 tbsp olive oil

With a fork, combine garlic, onion, bread crumbs, parsley, salt, red pepper, thyme, nutmeg, and lemon juice in a bowl. Stuff cavity of fish with the loosely combined mixture. Truss the cavity together with string. Place the whole stuffed fish on a moderately hot grill for approximately 8 to 10 minutes on each side.

Blend all of the sauce ingredients until smooth. Spoon over fish when serving. Add thin lemon slices to fish as a garnish.

(Serves 4)

◇ *Barbecued Halibut*

4 ½-lb halibut steaks
½ lb fresh mushrooms, sliced
3 tbsp butter

Marinade

2 tbsp chopped onion
2 tbsp chopped green pepper
2 tbsp oil
½ cup dry white wine
¼ cup soy sauce
½ cup chopped fresh tomatoes
1 garlic clove, finely chopped
2 tbsp fresh lemon juice
2 tbsp fresh ginger, finely grated

Sauté onion and green pepper in the oil. Add all remaining marinade ingredients except fish and mushrooms. Bring mixture to boil over high heat for 1 minute, set aside, and let cool. Place the steaks in a shallow dish and pour marinade over fish. Marinate at room temperature for an hour. Turn fillets occasionally. Drain fish, reserve marinade.

Sauté the mushrooms in 3 tablespoons of butter. Grill steaks 3 inches from mesquite coals for 4 to 5 minutes on each side. Baste with marinade and turn. Top with sautéed mushrooms.

(Serves 4)

◇ *Marinated Grilled Salmon*

4 1-in-thick salmon steaks
⅔ cup pimento olives, sliced

Marinade

⅓ cup dry sherry
⅓ cup olive oil

1 tsp salt
1 tbsp red wine vinegar
½ tsp dried anise or fresh chopped fennel

Set aside the pimento olives. Mix marinade ingredients and marinate salmon steaks. Let stand for several hours. Pat salmon steaks dry with cloth or paper towels before placing on hot mesquite grill.

Oil the grill to prevent sticking; with salmon this is especially important. Cook salmon steaks for about 5 to 6 minutes on each side. When ready to serve, spoon marinade over steaks, remove salmon from grill, garnish with sliced pimento olives, and serve.

(Serves 4)

◇ Sea Bass Steak

2 to 3 lb 1-in fillets sea bass

Sauce

¼ cup chopped fennel leaves or 2 tbsp dried fennel
½ cup dry white wine
2 tsp fresh lemon juice
salt and pepper
8 tbsp unsalted butter

Crush the fennel with the back of a knife. Insert a pinch of crushed fennel between the fillets of each fish. Refrigerate for 4 hours. Remove from refrigerator to allow fish to reach room temperature before grilling.

In a saucepan combine wine, remaining fennel, lemon juice, and salt and pepper to taste. Boil this mixture and reduce the sauce over medium heat to about 3 tablespoons. Allow butter to reach room temperature, then whisk in butter.

Place fish on rack 3 inches from mesquite coals. Cook on each side 4 to 5 minutes. To serve, place grilled fillets on platter and pour sauce over it.

(Serves 6)

◇ *Grilled Whole Sea Bass with Fresh Herbs*

1 3- to 4-lb sea bass
salt and pepper
1/4 cup olive oil
1/2 cup mixed fresh herbs, finely chopped (use parsley, tarra-
    gon, chives, and thyme)
1 1/2 cups dry bread crumbs

Split head and body of fish so that it will lie flat on the grill (make
sure not to divide fish). Sprinkle inside cavity with salt and pepper.
Then brush fish with oil, and press herb mixture firmly into both
sides of fish. Next press bread crumbs into flesh on both sides. Top
off with oil.

Grill on both sides, preferably in a hinged grill, turning until fish
turns crusty brown. It takes approximately 15 minutes per side with
this type and size of fish. The fish is done when the flesh reaches a
flaky consistency.

(Serves 4)

◇ *Shark Steak with Chili Butter*

2 8-oz shark steaks
2 tbsp olive oil
1 garlic clove, finely minced
3 tbsp butter
2/3 tbsp chili powder
1/2 tsp cumin
lime wedges
fresh sprigs of cilantro

Combine olive oil and garlic in dish large enough to hold the fish.
Place the shark steaks in dish and coat both sides with the garlic oil.
Mix chili powder and cumin into butter which has been softened to
room temperature.

Broil the steaks over the mesquite for between 3 to 5 minutes.
Turn the steaks, and brush with one-fourth of the chili butter. Broil

another 3 to 5 minutes. At serving time, top steaks with the remaining chili butter, and surround with lime wedges. Top off with sprigs of cilantro and serve.

(Serves 2)

◇ *Classic Swordfish*

6 6-oz swordfish steaks, ¾ inch thick
3 garlic cloves, crushed
2 tbsp fresh or dried rosemary
¼ cup olive oil
salt and pepper

Crush garlic and rosemary and add the olive oil to mixture. Brush both sides of steaks with seasoned oil mixture. Salt and pepper to taste. Grill the swordfish 3 inches from mesquite coals for about 4 minutes on each side.

(Serves 6)

◇ *Grilled Trout*

4 12-oz trout, cleaned
½ cup olive oil
salt and pepper
4 garlic cloves, finely chopped
¼ cup fresh parsley, finely chopped
3 tbsp dry white wine or vermouth

Brush the inside and outside of the trout with olive oil. Salt and pepper inside cavity of fish. Add the parsley, garlic, and wine to the remaining olive oil to make a relish. Spread the parsley relish on the insides of each trout.

Place each trout over a hot mesquite grill for 3½ minutes per side. Garnish with lemon and serve.

(Serves 4)

◇ *Grilled Tuna with Spiced Butter*

4 tuna fillets, approximately 8 oz each
1 cup unsalted butter, softened
2 tbsp minced cilantro
1 tsp jalapeño or serrano chili pepper, finely minced (For a milder sauce, remove seeds before mincing.)
2 tsp garlic, finely minced
1 tsp fresh ginger, finely minced, or powdered ginger

Place softened butter in mixing bowl and beat till fluffy. Blend in the cilantro, chili, garlic, and ginger. Spoon dollops of butter mixture onto waxed paper and refrigerate ahead of time for readied individual servings. Refrigerate.

Place fish on rack 3 inches from mesquite coals. Grill fish about 4 to 5 minutes on each side. Place dollops of spiced butter on the finished fillet, or warm the spiced butter and spoon over the cooked fillets.

(Serves 4)

9 ◇ Shellfish

Easy Ways to Grill Shellfish ◇ Mixed Shellfish Grill ◇
Chinese-Style Shellfish ◇ Grilled Dungeness Crab ◇ Grilled
Lobster Tails ◇ Grilled Oysters ◇ Grilled Shrimp ◇ Barbecued
Curry Shrimp ◇ Grilled Shrimp with Lime Butter ◇ Sesame
Shrimp ◇ Spicy Shrimp ◇ Grilled Squid

Cooking shellfish over mesquite presents a paradox: it involves both the simplest and the most difficult of cooking techniques.

It's the simplest in that it requires very little time on the grill in order to achieve truly magnificent results. It's the most difficult technique because delicious shellfish can be turned into dried disasters in a flash.

The key to grilling shellfish is experience. Through tasting, touching, and smelling the food as it grills, you'll learn how and when to remove the shellfish so that they're just underdone—but still cooking.

Like all foods on the grill, shellfish continue to cook even after being removed. The secret lies in learning how to time the perfect moment. A general rule of thumb is that shellfish are ready to be removed from the grill just as their flesh turns opaque, the sort of cloudy color which can only be spotted by keeping your eye watchfully on the grill. This, for large shrimp, can be as soon as 3 minutes for each side.

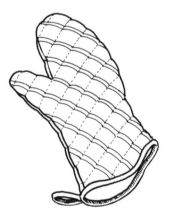

◇ Easy Ways to Grill Shellfish

Bacon Wraps

Pan-fry bacon until almost cooked. Wrap around scallops or shrimp, skewer, and grill. Grilling time is about 2 to 3 minutes.

Instant Marinade

In a small bowl combine 2 teaspoons of olive oil, 1 teaspoon lemon juice, 2 to 3 cloves crushed garlic, 2 tablespoons white wine, and soy sauce. Marinate scallops or shrimp for 1 hour. Grill on skewers, brushing with marinade continuously until cooked, about 2 to 4 minutes.

Curried Grill

Saturate raw shrimps or scallops in melted butter, then roll in curry powder. Skewer and grill over hot flame for 2 to 4 minutes. Don't overcook. Squeeze on a little lemon juice, and top with cilantro leaves before serving.

◇ Mixed Shellfish Grill

1 1½- to 2-lb. lobster
1 large crab
10 unshelled jumbo shrimp
10 oysters, shucked
10 mussels, shucked
¼ cup corn oil

Sauce

8 tbsp butter
4 garlic cloves, crushed
¼ cup white wine
¼ cup fresh parsley, finely chopped
salt
lime or lemon wedges

Cut lobster in half and eviscerate it. Separate crab from its top shell and clean. Brush the flesh with corn oil before setting on grill to ensure moisture. Rinse and skewer all of the smaller shellfish.

First cook the larger shellfish. The lobster requires 4 to 6 minutes per side. The crab requires 4 to 5 minutes per side. Large shrimp require 2 to 3 minutes per side. Oysters and mussels require 5 to 7 minutes. A good rule of thumb is that the bivalves are done once their flesh appears opaque.

In a saucepan fry the garlic in the butter over a medium fire. When the garlic turns golden brown, add white wine. Bring to a boil and reduce the liquid by one-quarter. Spoon hot garlic-wine butter over the shellfish just as they are removed from the grill and placed on a large serving platter. Sprinkle the chopped parsley over the shellfish, garnish with lemon wedges, and serve. Salt to taste.

(Serves 3 to 4)

◇ *Chinese-Style Shellfish*

>   *1 crab or lobster*
> *¼ cup peanut or corn oil*
>   *2 garlic cloves, crushed*
> *¼ cup scallions, finely chopped*
>   *2 tbsp soy sauce*
>   *1 tbsp freshly grated ginger*

Sauté garlic in oil until brown. Add chopped scallions, ginger, and soy sauce.

Grill shellfish for 5 to 6 minutes on each side. Place it on a platter, top off with the warm sauce mixture, and serve.

(Serves 2)

◇ *Grilled Dungeness Crab*

2 2-lb Dungeness crabs
8 tbsp clarified butter

Marinade

1 small garlic clove, crushed
¼ cup olive oil
Salt and pepper
2 tbsp fresh thyme, finely chopped, or 1 tsp dried thyme

Combine all marinade ingredients in a bowl. Halve crabs and pull off body shells. Clear crab meat of any debris. Rinse crab halves and crack legs and claws with a mallet. Then place the crab in bowl and marinate in refrigerator for 2 hours.

Grill the crab halves over a hot fire 4 to 5 minutes per side. Turn frequently. The crab is ready when the shell turns bright red. Serve with small dishes of melted butter for dipping.

(Serves 4)

◇ *Grilled Lobster Tails*

2 lobster tails
10 tbsp butter, melted
1 tsp paprika
salt and black pepper
2 garlic cloves, crushed
lemon quarters

Combine the butter with the paprika, salt, pepper, and garlic. Then brush half of the mixture on the flesh side of lobster. Place the flesh side down on the grill, and cook for approximately 4 to 6 minutes. Turn the lobster over, brush on the remainder of the butter mixture, and grill until flesh becomes opaque. Depending on the size of the fire, this usually takes 8 to 10 minutes. Garnish the tails with lemon quarters and serve.

(Serves 2)

◇ Grilled Oysters

24 oysters
4 shallots, finely chopped
8 tbsp unsalted butter
salt and freshly ground pepper
¼ cup lemon juice
bread crumbs
¼ cup Parmesan cheese, finely grated

Place oysters, rounded side down, on the grill for a few minutes until they pop open. Remove top shells. Mix chopped shallots with butter and dot each oyster with this mixture. Mix salt, pepper, lemon juice, bread crumbs, and Parmesan cheese in a small bowl. Top off each oyster with a generous pinch of this mixture. If you have a kettle-style grill, cover and cook until bread crumb mixture adheres to oysters. If you're using an open grill, cover oysters with a piece of aluminum foil or the top part of large boiling pot.

(Serves 6)

◇ Grilled Shrimp

2 lb large shrimp in shell
¼ cup sherry
¼ lb unsalted butter, melted
½ cup olive oil
1 tbsp shallots, minced
3 garlic cloves, finely chopped
1 tsp salt
2 tbsp lemon juice
¼ cup parsley, finely chopped
black pepper, freshly ground

Clean shrimp and marinate in the sherry for 30 minutes, turning at least once. Mix butter, olive oil, shallots, garlic, and salt. Add shrimp to the garlic-butter mixture, turning them frequently until they are completely coated. Add lemon juice, parsley and black pepper. Leave shrimp in marinade for another 30 minutes.

Place the shrimp on the grill. Set aside the remaining marinade in a small saucepan, keeping it warm by setting on the grill next to the shrimp. Grill shrimp 2 to 3 minutes per side or until shells turn bright pink. Remove from grill and pour on the garlic butter before serving.

(Serves 4)

◇ *Barbecued Curry Shrimp*

1½ lb unshelled large shrimp
1 tbsp curry powder
salt and pepper

Marinade

2 tbsp white wine
½ cup olive or peanut oil
2 tbsp melted butter
2 cloves garlic, finely chopped
1 tbsp curry powder

Combine white wine, oil, butter, garlic, and 1 tablespoon of curry powder in a bowl. Add shrimp and marinate for 1 hour. Remove shrimp from marinade and coat lightly with remaining curry. Sprinkle with salt and pepper. Broil over moderately high mesquite fire about 3 minutes on each side. Serve with chutney dip.

(Serves 2)

◇ *Grilled Shrimp with Lime Butter*

8–10 large unshelled shrimp
3 tbsp butter
2 tbsp lime juice
2 tbsp olive oil
cilantro sprigs
lime wedges

Melt butter in small saucepan. Stir in lime juice. Stir over a gentle heat and set aside, keeping the sauce warm. Halve the shrimp without removing the shell. Rub all over with olive oil.

Place the shrimp, flesh-side down, on grill to sear 1 minute. Turn shrimp over and continue cooking by placing a lid over shrimp, creating a smoking effect. After approximately 2 minutes place shrimp, flesh-side up, on plates. Top with lime butter, and garnish with lime wedges and cilantro sprigs.

(Serves 2)

◇ *Sesame Shrimp*

1 lb shelled large shrimp
3 garlic cloves, crushed
2 tbsp peanut oil
3 tbsp melted butter
black pepper, freshly ground
sesame seeds

Combine crushed garlic, oil, butter, and pepper. Marinate the shrimp in this mixture for 30 minutes. Toast the sesame seeds in a pan. Make sure to stir them continually over a low flame to avoid burning. Cool the seeds, and spread them over a large dinner plate. Roll the marinated shrimp in the sesame seeds until shrimps are lightly coated. Cook over moderately hot mesquite fire 3–4 minutes, turning frequently to avoid overcooking.

(Serves 2)

◇ *Spicy Shrimp*

2 lb unshelled large shrimp

Marinade

2 tbsp ketchup
1 cup olive oil

1/2 tsp cayenne pepper
1 tsp salt
1/2 tsp Tabasco sauce
2 garlic cloves, crushed
1/4 cup lemon juice
1 tsp oregano, crushed
1 tbsp Tabasco sauce
1/8 cup fresh orange juice

In a medium mixing bowl, combine all ingredients except the shrimp. Mix thoroughly with a whisk. Add shrimp and let marinate 1 to 2 hours. Set shrimp on medium hot grill. Cook for 2 to 3 minutes on each side. Baste shrimps continually while grilling. Dip sizzling hot shrimp in remaining sauce, and serve immediately.

(Serves 4)

◇ Grilled Squid

2 lb squid
8 tbsp butter, melted
1 garlic clove, crushed
lemon juice or soy sauce, to taste

Clean squid by cutting tentacles from head beyond the eyes and discarding the beak, a hard piece found in the middle of the tentacles. Then pull head out of the sac, drawing entrails with it, and discard. Rinse out the remaining matter in the sacs. Rinse tentacles and place on the grill for 2 to 3 minutes, turning frequently. Cut the sacs into 1/4-inch-wide rings. Place the rings on the grill, watching carefully to avoid overcooking. The squid cooks very rapidly and is done as soon as it turns opaque. Serve the squid with melted butter flavored with lemon juice or soy sauce.

(Serves 2)

10 ◇ Skewers and Kabobs

Sweet 'n' Sour Kabobs ◇ Spicy Beef Kabobs ◇ Stuffed Beef
Rolls on a Stick ◇ Chicken Kabobs ◇ Yakitori (Japanese
Chicken Stick) ◇ Fish Kabobs ◇ Satay Lamb ◇ Skewered Liver
◇ Spiced Chicken Livers on Skewers ◇ Pork Kabobs ◇
Skewered Turkey ◇ Mixed Skewered Vegetables

◇

To a lot of people the nicest thing about kabobs and skewers is how eye-appealing they are. I can see their point. There is something festive about the arrangement of bite-sized beef chunks, vegetables and fruit on a skewer. But to my mind what's really appealing about them is that there is no element of outdoor grilling that challenges the cook's imagination as much as the art of kabobs and skewers.

Ancient cooks probably realized this versatile method of grilling because it has been a popular way of food preparation for thousands of years. The chief advantages are that it allows the cook to serve a wide variety of different items together, along with the fact that the bite-size chunks cook faster and taste more tender.

The skewer is particularly useful in bringing together the juiciness of fresh fruit to flavor meats such as chicken and fish. The chief disadvantage is that it takes time in preparation because it's important to try and obtain uniformity in size when preparing the bite-size morsels. If some of your kabobs from the same skewer are overdone while others are just perfect, it's probably because of the difference in size between them. Be sure to check your kabobs carefully during cooking because unlike whole pieces of beef or fish the smaller chunks can burn surprisingly fast.

◇ Sweet 'n' Sour Kabobs

2 lb beef sirloin or fish fillets, cut into 2-in cubes
1 fresh pineapple, cubed
2 medium onions, quartered
2 green bell peppers, cut into 1-in squares

Marinade

salt and freshly ground pepper
1/4 cup white wine vinegar
1/2 cup fresh pineapple juice
2 tbsp molasses

In a large bowl combine cubed meat or fish and marinade ingredients. Toss gently and let stand at least 1 hour, turning occasionally. Strain the mixture in colander and reserve the marinade. Spear meat onto skewers and alternate with pineapple, onions, and green pepper pieces. Place on grill, turning frequently for about 3 to 5 minutes per side for beef and 3 to 4 minutes per side for fish. Remove kabobs from grill and dip into remaining marinade. Serve immediately.

(Serves 6)

◇ Spicy Beef Kabobs

1 1/2 lb flank steak, cut into 1-in-wide strips
1 large onion, cut into wedges
4 tbsp peanut butter

Marinade

1/4 cup soy sauce
4 tbsp vegetable oil
1/2 cup dry sherry
4 garlic cloves, minced
2 tsp dried red pepper flakes

In a medium bowl combine marinade ingredients. Add beef strips, and allow to marinate at least 1 hour or more. Remove the beef

111

strips, and set marinade aside. Thread the beef strips and onion wedges onto skewers, and grill for 2 to 3 minutes on each side. Turn and baste with marinade frequently. Warm the peanut butter until it melts. Remove the skewers from grill, and brush lightly with peanut butter. Serve immediately.

(Serves 4)

◇ *Stuffed Beef Rolls on a Stick*

1 lb beef sirloin, cut into 1-in-wide strips
1 cup stuffed olives, drained
1 can smoked oysters
1 large onion, cut into wedges
20–30 mushroom caps
¼ cup butter, melted
salt and pepper

Wrap a strip of beef around a stuffed olive, an oyster, an onion wedge, and a mushroom cap. Fasten each bundle with a toothpick, and brush with butter. Thread 3 or 4 bundles on each skewer, and place on grill, turning frequently for 6 to 8 minutes. Season with salt and pepper just before removing from the grill.

(Serves 4)

◇ *Chicken Kabobs*

2 whole chicken breasts, deboned
2 green or red bell peppers, cut in 1-in squares
1 garlic clove, crushed
15 mushroom caps, stems removed
2 large tomatoes, cut into wedges
¼ cup vinegar
1 tbsp paprika
1 tbsp salt
a few grains cayenne pepper or to taste
3 tbsp butter, melted

Cut chicken breasts into 1-inch cubes. Marinate chicken cubes, bell peppers, garlic, mushroom caps, and tomato wedges in the vinegar for 1 hour. Mix in the cayenne, paprika and salt. Drain liquid and reserve. Thread chicken, green peppers, mushrooms, and tomatoes alternately onto skewers. Set skewers on grill, turn frequently, and baste with remaining marinade and melted butter for approximately 2 to 3 minutes.

(Serves 2)

◇ Yakitori (Japanese Chicken Stick)

¾ cup dry sherry or sweet rice wine
1 cup soy sauce
5 tbsp sugar
4 large chicken breasts, boned and cut into 1-in cubes
1 green bell pepper, cut into 1-in squares
8 green onions, cut into 3-in segments
Japanese red pepper (sansho) *or cayenne pepper*

Combine ¼ cup wine, ½ cup soy sauce, and 4 tablespoons sugar in a large bowl. Add the chicken cubes, and let stand for 1 hour. Mix the remaining wine, soy sauce, and sugar in a small saucepan, and bring to a boil. Remove this basting liquid from the fire as soon as it reaches a rolling boil. Thread the bell pepper squares, chicken cubes, and green onions onto skewers. Set on grill over hot coals and cook about 2 to 3 minutes on each side. Baste continually. As you remove finished skewers from grill, dip each one in the remaining basting sauce and season lightly with Japanese red pepper or, if not available, cayenne pepper.

(Serves 4)

◇ *Fish Kabobs*

2 lb swordfish or halibut steaks
2 large zucchini squash, in ½-in slices
1 pt cherry tomatoes
1 cup dry vermouth
2 tbsp black pepper, freshly ground

Cut fish into 1-inch cubes. Alternate pieces of fish, squash, and cherry tomatoes onto skewers. Add black pepper to vermouth for an instant basting sauce. Brush fish and vegetables with the vermouth, and set the skewered kabobs on a medium hot grill. Turn often while basting until fish cubes become completely opaque—approximately 2 to 3 minutes for each side.

(Serves 6)

◇ *Satay Lamb*

1½ lb lean boneless lamb
salt and pepper
¾ cup soy sauce
2 tbsp lemon juice
2 garlic cloves, crushed
2 onions, thinly sliced

Cut the lamb into 1-inch cubes. Season with salt and pepper. Combine about ½ cup of soy sauce with the lemon juice in a large bowl. Crush the garlic and add it to the marinade. Add the lamb cubes and marinate the lamb for at least 2 hours. Thread the lamb chunks on skewers, and grill over mesquite for approximately 5 to 8 minutes, turning occasionally to avoid burning. Thinly slice the onions for garnish and sprinkle meat with remainder of the soy sauce just before removing the lamb skewers from the grill.

(Serves 4)

◇ *Skewered Liver*

1 lb chicken livers or calf liver
6 bacon strips, cut into 3-in segments

Halve chicken livers or cut calf liver into 1-inch cubes. Then wrap
the cubes of liver in uncooked bacon strips. Spear several of these
bacon-wrapped morsels onto skewers and grill. Turn every few
minutes until bacon is crisp.

(Serves 4)

◇ *Spiced Chicken Livers on Skewers*

1 lb chicken livers, halved
salt and pepper
1 tsp cinnamon
¼ cup butter, melted
¼ cup dry sherry

Season the halved chicken livers with salt and pepper and a sprin-
kling of cinnamon. Skewer the livers and brush with butter. Place on
grill, turning every 3 to 4 minutes. Continue brushing with melted
butter until livers are browned on outside. Liver should still be
slightly pink inside when done. Remove skewers from grill, dip in
sherry, and return to grill for a minute or two. Serve immediately.

(Serves 2 to 3)

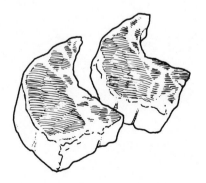

◇ *Pork Kabobs*

2 lb boneless pork, fat removed
1 medium eggplant
2 large green apples
12 small onions
3 tbsp olive oil

Marinade

½ cup olive oil
3 tbsp lemon juice
3 tbsp red wine vinegar
1 tbsp curry powder
2 tbsp rosemary, crushed
2 garlic cloves, crushed
1 tsp salt

Cut pork into 1-inch cubes and set aside. Combine marinade ingredients, add pork, and refrigerate overnight in a covered bowl. Cut the eggplant into cubes just slightly larger than the pork. Core the apples and cut horizontally 1-inch cubes. Fry the small onions in olive oil for 3 to 4 minutes. Add the apples, eggplant, and onions to pork, and toss thoroughly. Alternately spear the ingredients on skewers. Set aside the remaining marinade. Place over gray mesquite coals, turning frequently at least 3 to 4 times. Cook for about 8 to 10 minutes.

(Serves 4)

◇ *Skewered Turkey*

1 turkey breast half
4 tbsp butter, melted

Marinade

⅓ cup corn oil
¼ cup soy sauce
½ cup dry vermouth

2 tbsp lemon juice
1½ tbsp fresh ginger, finely grated
3 garlic cloves, crushed
1 tbsp black pepper, freshly ground

Skin and cut turkey breast into 1-inch cubes, and set aside. Combine marinade ingredients in a large mixing bowl. Place turkey cubes in marinade, and let stand in the refrigerator for approximately 4 hours. Before grilling, remove the turkey cubes from the refrigerator, and let stand until they reach room temperature. Skewer cubes tightly together. Place on grill over a medium fire for about 10 to 15 minutes, turning frequently to avoid burning. Remove from grill, brush lightly with butter, and serve.

(Serves 4)

◇ *Mixed Skewered Vegetables*

2 green or red peppers, cut into 1-in squares
20 mushroom caps
purple onions, cut into 1-in pieces
1 pt cherry tomatoes
1 medium-size zucchini, sliced into 1-in cubes
1 small to medium-size eggplant, cut into 1-in cubes
½ cup olive oil
salt and pepper
1 tsp dried oregano
1 tsp dried basil

Place vegetables on skewers in a colorful pattern. Skewer the mushrooms through their caps, the zucchini through the skin. Use the firmer vegetables, like the onions and peppers, to support the more delicate ones, like the tomatoes. Mix the olive oil with salt, pepper, oregano, and basil to make a simple but delicious marinade. Place the vegetables on the grill over a low fire. When the peppers and onions are soft, the vegetables are ready to eat.

(Serves 4)

11 ◇ Vegetables and Side Dishes

Green Bean Bacon Rolls ◇ Barbecued Herbed Carrots ◇
Mexican-Style Grilled Corn ◇ Grilled Whole Eggplant ◇
Eggplant Italiano ◇ Stuffed Mushrooms ◇ Mixed Grilled
Peppers ◇ Grilled Potato ◇ Tasty Roast Potatoes ◇ Pumpkin
Kabobs ◇ Ratatouille Cooked in Foil ◇ Grilled Whole
Tomatoes ◇ Skewered Bacon and Water Chestnuts ◇ Grilled
Yams ◇ Grilled Zucchini ◇ Homemade Barbecue Beans ◇
Simple Chili Beans ◇ Quick and Easy Bean Salad ◇ Cornbread
◇ Cucumber Relish ◇ Stuffed Baked Potatoes ◇ Oil and
Vinegar Potato Salad ◇ Summer Salad

◇

All too frequently people think of vegetables as something to be boiled or fried. But the devotees of the barbecue know the wealth of flavor offered by the vegetable that is allowed to spend some time on the grill.

This is all the more true when the grill is fired by mesquite. The delicate, inimitable flavor that mesquite grilling lends to all kinds of vegetables—including squash, corn, zucchini, tomatoes, and eggplant—is the perfect accompaniment to the outdoor meal.

There is no great secret involved in turning out tasty vegetables on the outdoor grill. Simply bear in mind that cooking vegetables in this manner requires careful basting and frequent turning so that they cook at an even rate. Here, however, we should distinguish between thick- and thin-skinned vegetables.

With thick-skinned vegetables such as eggplant and zucchini it's best to coat them lightly with oil before putting them on the grill. Then baste occasionally over medium fire.

The more fleshy type of vegetables such as tomatoes must be scored to keep their skins from bursting and their juices from escaping into the hot coals.

The grill's versatility is very evident when you are cooking vegetables. It can be used for steaming or direct grilling, or you can place the vegetables in foil and cook them directly on the coals. In addition, the most wonderful aromas can be created by adding just a pinch of herbs or a dash of lemon juice or wine to your vegetables before or during their cooking.

◇ *Green Bean Bacon Rolls*

1 lb green beans
salt
8 slices bacon
1 tbsp rosemary, crushed
black pepper, freshly ground

Trim ends off beans and blanch in salted water. Make four rolls as follows. For each roll, place 2 bacon slices side by side, slightly overlapping. Place about ¼ pound of green beans at the end of the bacon slices. Carefully roll up the beans into a tidy bundle. Sprinkle with a pinch of rosemary and pepper. Wrap each roll in aluminum foil, and seal tightly. Place on grill or directly in the mesquite coals. Turn often and cook for 15 to 20 minutes or until bacon is done.

(Serves 4)

◇ *Barbecued Herbed Carrots*

1 lb baby carrots
4 tbsp butter
1 tsp dry thyme
3–4 tbsp water
salt

Wash and peel carrots. Brush carrots with butter, and place them on aluminum foil. Sprinkle on thyme, water, and salt to taste. Wrap up the carrots, and place them on the grill. Turn occasionally, cooking for 1 hour or until carrots are tender.

(Serves 4)

◇ *Mexican-Style Grilled Corn*

4 ears corn, unshucked
juice of 2 limes
2 tsp chili powder or to taste
1 tsp cayenne pepper (optional)

This wonderful version of grilled corn is sold all along the highways of Mexico at makeshift fast-food stands. Turn the husks back without tearing from the cob. Remove as much of the silk as possible, dip in water, and replace the husks.

Place on grill and let ears toast until the kernels begin to brown, turning often. Just before serving remove husks and sear on grill for a couple of minutes, turning often. Squeeze lime juice over corn, and sprinkle with chili powder to taste. If you prefer your corn a little more picante, sprinkle a little cayenne pepper over the corn as well.

(Serves 4)

◇ Grilled Whole Eggplant

1 large eggplant or 4 small eggplants
¼ cup olive oil
2 tbsp lemon juice
1 clove garlic, crushed
salt and freshly ground pepper
¾ tsp cumin

Eggplant is best if grilled in its own skin. Smaller eggplants of the Oriental variety are most desirable for grilling whole. Place eggplants on grill, rotating every few minutes. Eggplant is done when it becomes black, blistered, and soft. Cut lengthwise in half. Scoop the flesh into a medium bowl. Mash eggplant, add olive oil, lemon juice, garlic, salt, pepper, and cumin. Let cool. Serve at room temperature.

(Serves 4)

◇ Eggplant Italiano

2 medium-sized eggplants

Marinade

½ cup olive oil
1 garlic clove, crushed
1 tsp paprika

black pepper, freshly ground
1/2 tsp oregano
salt

Combine marinade ingredients. Prepare eggplants by peeling and cutting crosswise into 1/2-inch slices. Marinate the eggplant for 15 minutes. Broil the slices over a low mesquite fire for 8 to 10 minutes on each side, or until they are well browned.

Variations: Asparagus and zucchini are also excellent over mesquite.

(Serves 4)

◇ *Stuffed Mushrooms*

24 large mushroom caps
salt and pepper

Stuffing

2 tbsp mixed herbs (thyme, sweet basil, and oregano)
1/2 cup bread crumbs
4 tbsp parmesan cheese, finely grated
4 tbsp softened butter
1/4 cup parsley, finely chopped

Mix stuffing ingredients with a fork. Salt and pepper mushroom caps to taste and fill with stuffing. Wrap the mushroom caps securely in foil. Place on a hot grill for 5 minutes, turn, and cook on the other side for additional 5 minutes. Serve hot.

(Serves 6)

◇ *Mixed Grilled Peppers*

3 large green bell peppers
3 large red bell peppers
1/4 cup olive oil
3/4 cup vinegar
salt and pepper

Roast peppers whole on the grill until their skins blister. Turn frequently so that all sides are roasted on grill. Peel the skins, and remove the seeds and stems. Slice into strips and coat with olive oil, vinegar, salt, and pepper. Serve at room temperature, or chill and serve as a salad.

(Serves 4)

◇ Grilled Potato

> 4 large potatoes
> ¼ cup olive oil
> salt
> pepper
> 2 tbsp tarragon

Cut each potato into about six wedges. Soak wedges in ice water for about 30 minutes. Rinse twice to wash away excess potato starch. Parboil or steam the potato wedges until tender but not flaky. Place potatoes in a shallow container, and add a light, even coating of oil. Salt and pepper wedges, and grill wedges over moderately hot mesquite fire until brown and crispy. Brush potatoes with olive oil, and sprinkle with tarragon.

(Serves 4)

◇ Tasty Roast Potatoes

> 4 potatoes
> 4 tsp butter
> salt and pepper
> 1 teaspoon tarragon, crushed
> 2 garlic cloves, crushed
> sour cream (optional)

Wash potatoes. Slice in half lengthwise. Butter flesh sides, and season with salt, pepper, and crushed tarragon. Spread the crushed garlic cloves between the potato halves, and wrap in aluminum foil. Place the potatoes horizontally on coals, or directly on grill. Roast for about 1 hour, turning several times. Serve with sour cream (optional).

(Serves 4)

◇ *Pumpkin Kabobs*

> *1 lb pumpkin, peeled and cubed into 1½-in portions*
> *12 cherry tomatoes*
> *2 medium potatoes, in 1-in cubes*
> *4 tbsp softened butter*
> *1 tsp tarragon, crushed*
> *1 tsp oregano, crushed*
> *salt and freshly ground pepper*

Parboil pumpkin and potato cubes for 5 minutes. Thread pumpkin cubes, tomatoes, and potatoes chunks on skewers. Mash the tarragon and oregano into the butter, and melt over low flame. Brush the skewers with herb butter, and season with salt and pepper. Grill for 5 to 6 minutes on each side, basting frequently until golden brown. Brush with herb butter before serving.

(Serves 4)

◇ *Ratatouille Cooked in Foil*

> *1 large eggplant*
> *1½ tsp salt*
> *½ cup olive oil*
> *3 large garlic cloves, crushed*
> *2 purple onions, thickly sliced*
> *2 green peppers, julienned*
> *5 tomatoes, peeled, seeded, and diced*
> *5 zucchinis, julienned*
> *1 tbsp black pepper, freshly ground*
> *2 tbsp fresh basil and fresh oregano, finely chopped*
> *2–3 tbsp lemon juice or vinegar*

Cut the eggplant into ½-inch cubes. Sprinkle generously with salt, and allow the juices to drain in a colander for about 30 minutes.

Combine all of the ingredients in a large mixing bowl, and toss well. Pour the combination onto a large sheet of aluminum foil. Double-wrap the foil securely around the ratatouille, and place on the grill or directly into the coals for 15 to 20 minutes.

(Serves 4)

◇ *Grilled Whole Tomatoes*

6 tomatoes
olive oil
salt and freshly ground black pepper
2 tbsp fresh basil, finely chopped
2 tbsp grated parmesan cheese

Place large, firm, whole tomatoes on the grill, rotating them every few minutes until they are soft. Place them on platter, and cut them in half. Dribble olive oil on open faces of tomatoes, then sprinkle salt, pepper, fresh basil, and grated parmesan over the tomatoes while they're still steaming hot.

(Serves 3)

◇ *Skewered Bacon and Water Chestnuts*

1 8-oz can pineapple chunks
1 6-oz can water chestnuts
4 bacon slices, lightly cooked, cut in 1-in-long strips
½ cup red wine
½ cup pineapple juice

Drain water chestnuts and pineapple chunks, reserve pineapple juice. Tightly wrap a 1-inch bacon strip around a water chestnut. Place wrapped chestnut on skewer. Add a chunk of pineapple and alternate water chestnuts and pineapple several times. Mix pineapple juice and wine in a shallow dish. Place skewers in the liquid. Allow to stand 1 hour. Drain. Reserve liquid. Place skewers over medium hot fire, turning and basting with the marinade until bacon is crispy.

(Serves 2)

◇ *Grilled Yams*

4 yams
4 tbsp butter, melted
¼ cup brown sugar
1 tbsp cinnamon
¼ tsp nutmeg

The smaller, sweeter yams are best for grilling, so try and find this type. Parboil the yams for 10 to 15 minutes. Heat on the grill over the mesquite. Dip yams in melted butter, then in brown sugar. To serve, sprinkle with cinnamon and nutmeg.

(Serves 4)

◇ *Grilled Zucchini*

2 large or 6 small zucchinis
2 tbsp butter
salt and pepper

Brush zucchinis with butter, and place directly on grill or grill in a wire basket, or double-wrap individually in foil and place onto the hot coals directly. For larger zucchinis, cut into strips or cube and skewer. Place the strips or cubes on the grill, and turn often to avoid burning. Once the vegetables soften, they are ready. Brush with butter, season with salt and pepper, and serve.

(Serves 2)

◇ *Homemade Barbecue Beans*

2 lb Great Northern beans
8 cups water
2 cups Miller Lite Beer
½ lb salt pork or bacon cut into cubes
⅓ to ½ cup molasses
1 small onion, diced
1 tsp dry mustard
¼ tsp dried ginger
1 16-oz can tomato sauce
½ cup ketchup

Soak the beans overnight in the water and beer. Use a 4-quart pot with a tightly fitted lid. Drain beans and reserve water for later use. Alternate layers of pork and beans, starting with the beans at the bottom of pot. Add the molasses, onion, spices, tomato sauce, ketchup, and reserved water. Cover tightly and cook 6 to 8 hours, stirring every 20 to 30 minutes, adding water as needed.

(Serves 8)

◇ *Simple Chili Beans*

1 lb pinto beans
1 tbsp lard or bacon fat
3 garlic cloves, finely chopped
2 celery stalks, finely diced
1 small onion, finely chopped
1 tsp oregano
¼ tsp cumin
6 tbsp chili powder
salt and pepper
2 cups tomato sauce
3 tbsp red wine

Cook the beans slowly in 4 cups of water for about 2–3 hours or until they are just tender. While the beans are cooking, brown the garlic, celery, and onions in the bacon fat. Add the spices, tomato sauce, and red wine. Simmer for 1 hour. Then add the beans, and simmer for an additional 30 minutes.

(Serves 4)

◇ Quick and Easy Bean Salad

1 can garbanzo beans, drained and washed
1 can kidney beans, drained and washed
2 garlic cloves, minced
1/2 cup red wine vinegar
1 tbsp dried oregano, crushed
1/2 cup olive oil
1/2 medium-size onion, finely chopped
1 can black olives
4 tbsp parsley, finely chopped

Combine all ingredients in a mixing bowl. Gently toss to allow the flavors to mingle. Refrigerate for 3–4 hours. Serve at room temperature.

(Serves 4)

◇ Cornbread

1 1/2 cups yellow cornmeal
1/2 cup sifted all-purpose flour
1 tsp salt
1 tsp sugar
3 tsp baking powder
1 cup milk
3 eggs, well beaten
1/4 cup cream
1/3 cup melted butter

Sift dry ingredients into a mixing bowl. Add milk and eggs to dry ingredients, and beat with a wooden spoon. Beat in cream and melted butter. Pour into an 8½ × 11-inch buttered pan, and bake in a preheated oven at 400°F for 15 to 20 minutes. Cut into squares and serve.

(Serves 6 to 8)

◇ *Cucumber Relish*

> 1¾ *cups cucumber, finely chopped*
> ½ *cup carrot, finely grated*
> ¼ *cup onion, minced*
> 2 *tsp salt*
> ¼ *cup vinegar*
> ½ *tsp sugar*
> ¾ *tsp dill seeds*
> 2 *tbsp fresh cilantro, finely chopped*

Combine all ingredients in a bowl. Toss to mix well. Spoon relish into a jar. Cover jar and chill in refrigerator overnight to blend flavors.

(Makes about 2 cups)

◇ *Stuffed Baked Potatoes*

> 4 *large potatoes*
> 1 *cup cheddar cheese, grated*
> 1 *cup sour cream*
> 1 *small onion, finely diced*
> 1 *tsp nutmeg, finely grated*
> *salt and pepper to taste*

Bake potatoes for 1 hour or until tender at 375°F. Lengthwise, cut a portion off the top of the potatoes about ¼ inch deep. Scoop out as much of the potato from the skin as possible to make a "boat." Place the potato in a mixing bowl. Add ¾ cup grated cheese, sour cream, onions, nutmeg, salt and pepper to taste. Mash this mixture together until it is smooth. Return mixture to shelled potatoes, top with remaining cheese, and bake for another 15 minutes.

(Serves 4)

◇ Oil and Vinegar Potato Salad

> 8 medium-size potatoes
> 2 garlic cloves, crushed
> 6 tbsp olive oil
> 1 tsp salt
> 1 tsp ground pepper
> 3 tbsp wine vinegar
> 2/3 cup green onions, diced
> 4 tsp dried tarragon
> 4 slices well-cooked bacon, crumbled

Boil potatoes in their jackets until done. Peel potatoes as quickly as possible after cooling and slice fairly thin. Add garlic, olive oil, salt, pepper, and vinegar, and allow the potatoes to marinate for 20 to 30 minutes. Before serving, add the green onions, tarragon, and bacon bits, and toss gently. Serve chilled or at room temperature.

(Serves 4)

◇ Summer Salad

> 1 whole green pepper
> 1 whole red pepper
> 1 cucumber
> 1 avocado
> 10 cherry tomatoes
> ½ cup cilantro, chopped
> 3 garlic cloves, crushed
> ½ cup red wine vinegar
> ⅛ cup olive oil
> salt and pepper to taste
> 2 tbsp fresh basil, finely chopped

Cut all the vegetables except the tomatoes into ½-inch pieces. Combine vegetables in a mixing bowl. Add cilantro, garlic, vinegar, olive oil, salt and pepper to taste. Gently toss and chill. Halve the cherry tomatoes and add to salad just before serving. Sprinkle the fresh basil over the salad and serve.

(Serves 2)

12 ◇ Fruits

Grilled Mixed Fruit ◇ Apples in Foil ◇ Apple on a Stick ◇
Whole Roasted Bananas ◇ Drunken Bananas ◇ Grilled
Grapefruit ◇ Grand Marnier Oranges ◇ Orange and Banana
Kabobs ◇ Grilled Peaches ◇ Chocolate Stuffed Pears ◇ Grilled
Pineapple Upside-Down Cake ◇ Spiced Plums

◇

Fruits are not usually thought of as appropriate for barbecuing. In fact, most people are surprised when they see me arranging different kinds of fruit on my outdoor grill. The truth of the matter is that most fleshy fruits, including oranges and grapefruit, make great companions to a mesquite-grilled feast.

The unique, distinctive flavor of mesquite—delicately smoky, subtly aromatic—blends especially well with the sweet, strong flavors of most fruits. Mesquite does not overpower fruits the way some other stronger-flavored types of cooking fuel do.

Like the vegetables cooked over mesquite, fruits show a similar adaptability to the many varieties of cooking techniques. For instance, bananas and pineapple can be placed on the grill directly, or they can be soaked in liqueurs and spices, then wrapped in foil, and placed directly on the coals.

To make delectable desserts and side dishes, the fruits should be prepared for ready eating (cored, stemmed, or cubed) before wrapping. Then they should be allowed to steam in their own juices. For no-nonsense results, add a chunk of butter and a pinch of sugar to almost any fruit, wrap it in foil, and place on the coals for a delightful instant dessert or side dish. To my mind, there is no more delicious outdoor treat to top off your mesquite-grilled barbecue.

◇ Grilled Mixed Fruit

1½ lb mixed fruit (peaches, apricots, pineapple, pears, apples,
    plums, and cherries)
¼ cup sugar
lemon juice
  3 tbsp butter, melted (optional)

Cut fruit up into large pieces so it will hold up on skewers. Sprinkle
the apples and pears with a little lemon juice to prevent discoloring.
Alternate the fruit on skewers. Grill over medium fire, turning the
skewers frequently. Sprinkle with sugar to carmelize. If you don't
care for the carmelized effect, baste the fruit skewers with a mixture
of melted butter with orange or lemon juice.

(Serves 4)

◇ Apples in Foil

4 red or green apples
½ cup butter
4 tsp cinnamon
½ cup white or brown sugar
¼ cup raisins
whipped cream

Wash and core apples. Fill insides with butter, raisins, cinnamon, and
sugar. Double wrap the apples. Place the tightly wrapped apples into
the coals for approximately 30 minutes. Top with whipped cream
and serve.

(Serves 4)

◇ Apple on a Stick

2 medium-size apples
2 tbsp butter, melted
1 tsp cinnamon
⅛ cup brown sugar, packed

Wash apples and place on skewer. Place apples on grill directly over the coals until tender, 20 to 30 minutes, turn. Peel off skin and dip apple in melted butter. Sprinkle with cinnamon and roll in brown sugar. Then rotate it slowly for 10 minutes over heat until sugar carmelizes. Cool and serve on skewer.

(Serves 2)

◇ *Whole Roasted Bananas*

4 bananas
4 tsp rum
4 tsp cinnamon

Slit banana skins, and sprinkle the inside of each banana with 1 teaspoon of rum and 1 teaspoon of cinnamon. Reseal the skins with toothpicks and place on grill, cooking for 10 minutes and turning once.

(Serves 4)

◇ *Drunken Bananas*

6 bananas, peeled
1/3 cup brown sugar
1/4 cup dark rum
1/2 tbsp cinnamon
3 tbsp butter
3 tbsp flaked coconut (optional)

Place the bananas on a large sheet of foil. Sprinkle brown sugar, rum, cinnamon, and chunks of butter on top of the bananas. Seal the foil wrap into a packet and place on the grill. Cook 10 to 15 minutes. Turn every 5 minutes. Serve with flaked coconut.

(Serves 6)

◇ Grilled Grapefruit

3 grapefruit
1/2 cup brown sugar
1/3 cup softened butter
6 tbsp rum

Halve grapefruits. Slice off rounded bottom so grapefruit can stand on its own. Loosen the grapefruit sections with a knife. Combine the brown sugar, butter, and rum into a paste. Coat tops of the grapefruit heavily with this mixture. Place grapefruit sugar-side up on grill about 6 to 8 inches above the mesquite. Adjust your grill or remove some of the coals if the fire is too hot. Grill for 10 minutes without turning. If grapefruit doesn't swell up, leave on grill until top is hot to the touch.

(Serves 3)

◇ Grand Marnier Oranges

6 large oranges
1/2 cup brown sugar
1/2 cup raisins
3 tsp cinnamon
6 tbsp butter, melted
6 tbsp Grand Marnier or Orange Liqueur (optional)

Peel the oranges, cut into crosswise slices, and remove pits. Layer the slices and sprinkle a little brown sugar, raisins, and cinnamon in between each layer. Then re-form the oranges into their original shape. Pour 1 tablespoon of liqueur and 1 tablespoon of butter over each orange, and wrap in aluminum foil tightly to avoid leakage. Place oranges directly on top of mesquite. Turn after 6 minutes. Cook another 5 minutes or until soft.

(Serves 6)

◇ *Orange and Banana Kabobs*

1 can mandarin orange slices, drained
3 bananas, sliced 1-inch thick
3 tbsp Grand Marnier
2 tbsp corn syrup
½ cup chocolate chips
coconut, flaked (optional)

Dip banana and orange segments in Grand Marnier and let stand for about 5 minutes. Drain fruit. Reserve juices. Skewer fruit, brush with corn syrup, and grill for a few minutes on each side. In a small saucepan, melt chocolate in reserved juices. Place the skewers on a serving plate, and pour the orange-chocolate sauce over the fruit kabobs.

Variation: Coconut can also be sprinkled on top of kabobs.

(Serves 4)

◇ *Grilled Peaches*

6 medium-size peaches
4 tbsp butter
6 tbsp brown sugar
sour cream or vanilla yogurt
flavored liqueur or raspberry preserves

Peel and halve 6 firm peaches. Remove pit and brush all over with 2 tablespoons of melted butter. Place cut side down, and grill for 2 to 3 minutes on each side or until lightly brown. In a small pan placed on the grill, melt 2 tablespoons butter, and stir in 6 tablespoons brown sugar. Serve peaches topped with melted brown sugar mixture, sour cream or yogurt, flavored liqueur, or a spoonful of raspberry preserves.

(Serves 3)

◇ *Chocolate Stuffed Pears*

> *4 pears*
> *¼ cup ground toasted almonds*
> *2 tbsp sugar*
> *2 tbsp butter*
> *1 egg yolk*
> *½ cup chocolate chips*

Wash and core pears. Mix almonds, sugar, butter, and egg yolk to form a paste. Add chocolate chips. Stuff center of pears with mixture. Wrap stuffed pears individually in foil. Place pears upright directly on hot coals and rotate regularly for 15 minutes.

(Serves 4)

◇ *Grilled Pineapple Upside-Down Cake*

> *1 pound cake*
> *1 16-oz can sliced pineapple, drained*
> *½ cup butter*
> *2 cups brown sugar*
> *¼ cup rum*
> *whipped cream (optional)*

This dessert can be prepared in advance. Because of its packaging it's great for camping and picnics.

Slice the pound cake in half lengthwise. If the cake is rounded at the top, trim it flat. Fashion aluminum foil into two separate "boats" deep enough to accommodate each layer, and grease bottoms with butter. Place pineapple in each foil boat. Layer each boat with pineapple, brown sugar, and rum. Then place each cake layer on top of pineapple slices. Wrap foil to cover. Place on grill, pineapple-side down, for 10 to 15 minutes. Serve in packets, or place upside down on plates and top with whipped cream.

(Serves 4–6)

◇ *Spiced Plums*

8 plums
⅓ cup brown sugar
½ tbsp ground allspice
4 tbsp kirsch

Wash plums, halve them, and remove pits. Place plums skin-side down on a sheet of foil. Sprinkle lightly with brown sugar and allspice. Pour ½ teaspoon of kirsch on top of each plum half. Wrap twice in aluminum foil, and set on top of grey coals. Cook for 10 to 15 minutes.

(Serves 4)

Index

Catalog

If you are interested in a list of fine Paperback
books, covering a wide range of subjects
and interests, send your name and address,
requesting your free catalog, to:

McGraw-Hill Paperbacks
1221 Avenue of Americas
New York, N.Y. 10020